FAULKNER

FAULKNER

Conflict and Consent
in Irish Politics

by

DAVID BLEAKLEY

MOWBRAYS

LONDON & OXFORD

© 1974 *David Bleakley*

Printed in Northern Ireland at The Universities Press, Belfast

ISBN O 264 66227 X

First published 1974 *by*
A. R. Mowbray Co. Ltd., The Alden Press,
Osney Mead, Oxford, OX2 0EG

to Winnie, my wife,
with affection and gratitude
for our *safari bora*

ACKNOWLEDGEMENTS
TO PHOTOGRAPHS

1 Robert J. Anderson & Co.
2 Associated Press
3 Belfast News Letter
4 Belfast Telegraph
5 The Northern Whig
6 Portadown Times
7 The Press Association
8 Leslie Stuart
9 The Times
10 Topix

Contents

Introduction

When I was invited to write a biography of Brian Faulkner the difficulties were obvious. The subject was still in mid-career, with substantial question marks over his future. Indeed, he had recently started on a new political course which was to prove as hazardous as it was innovatory.

Given the uncertainties of North Irish politics, there was no guarantee that he would even stay in office long enough to complete anything like a full term (in fact, he stayed five months), or even establish the new system of partnership government to which he had made a personal commitment.

But on reflection, I came to recognise that what was happening to Irish politics, and Brian Faulkner's position, particularly with the test of a new political system in Northern Ireland in January 1974, was special in that his had been a central presence throughout the Ulster crisis. For this reason an examination of his life and times brings us to the heart of things; but he will stand on his own account as a subject for biography. A man of many parts, yet largely unknown, he has been weaving his way through the labyrinth of Anglo-Irish politics for twenty-five years. For some, he is an Irish Pheonix, supreme in survival politics; for others, he has chameleon tendencies, insufficiently committed; and for his followers, he symbolises the basic Ulster Unionist position. But to all, he insists on remaining a remote figure, given much to public comment, but not to private revelation.

My approach to the task has been based on a considerable period of community involvement, and, in particular, as a Labour member of the Northern Ireland Parliament and the new Assembly. We contested our first General Election in the same year (1949), and during my time in the Ulster House of Commons I was required to 'shadow' Faulkner from the Labour benches in his work as Minister of Home Affairs and Minister of Commerce. Later, as a Labour representative,

I joined his first Government as Minister of Community Relations, and in 1973 we were each elected to the Northern Ireland Assembly. During these years we got to know each other as Parliamentary colleagues and, though politically opposed (and though we never rode to hounds together!), we have shared a good many political occasions. Even so, in more than two decades of contact it has not been easy to get to know the essential Faulkner.

Research on Ulster's first Chief Minister is made more difficult by his reluctance to put pen to paper. He has kept no diaries and apart from a few articles has done no writing for publication. He has been, however, a prolific and careful speech-maker, particularly in Parliament, and for those seeking evidence of the style and content of his speeches, the Northern Ireland Hansard provides a ready source. Many of his most important contributions have been given at regular intervals during his career at monthly meetings of East Down Unionists or at Orange gatherings. Again, on all these occasions the preparation has been careful and local editors have been well prepared in advance.

In this respect Irish politicians are fortunate. Politics really matter to Irish newspapers and political journalism is of a high order. Because of this, the press of the island, with pen and camera, have created a formidable library of politics which repays study. Based in Northern Ireland are the 'Belfast Telegraph', 'Belfast News-Letter', and the 'Irish News', while from the South come the 'Irish Times, 'Irish Independent', and the 'Irish Press'. These six provide a rich store of daily record and comment; it is little wonder that politics in Ireland is still the greatest national pastime. Fortunately for Faulkner, his wife was a journalist and her professional skill has accumulated over the years a well organised library of speeches and press cuttings, equalled by few of his colleagues. She has kept a good family picture album, to which she gave me generous access.

I have also been able to draw on personal sources of information. Throughout the events related I have known most of the chief participants and I have had the use of political diaries and papers gathered during the period. Impressions have emerged which may throw new light on some of the events. Use has also been made of official sources which are not readily available to those outside the immediate service of a parliamentary library. Here Northern Ireland is favoured. The Stormont library is one of the best of its kind, with a considerable collection of historical material, backed by an enthusiastic and skilled library staff. But this book is in no way an 'official' biography; the subject was aware that it was being written, but basically there the matter ended.

And how long has it taken to write? In a sense the 'writing' has been going on for twenty-five years of public life in Northern Ireland, as Protestant and Catholic together, we have searched for a *via media*. Perhaps, indeed, it all began way back in the early 1930s when my trade union father took me as a boy on many a tour of political meetings held by the local establishment. And always the advice was the same: 'Son, don't believe a word these fellows say. They're all the same—a cynical bunch.' I used to wonder what 'cynical' meant, but I got the drift. Later on, I came across that more precise Irish definition of a cynic: 'A man who knows the price of everything and the value of nothing.' All in all, they were sombre warnings.

But my own subsequent experience has tempered my judgement of Irish politics. Its practitioners are no more open to the scorn of Wilde's dictum than any other group who pursue a demanding calling. Certainly, what cannot be denied is that the life of politics in Ireland is indeed exacting and no more so than in the Northern Province. How exacting, I hope this book will help to reveal.

CHAPTER ONE

Subject of Controversy

Brian Faulkner's favourite book is *The Experiences of an Irish R.M.* It is an apt choice; these immortal tales, some humorous, some tragic, have a special appeal for public men caught up in the rich variety of Irish country life. What rural MP reading Somerville and Ross has not encountered something of the same cut-and-thrust in the daily constituency round?

It is little wonder that Brian Faulkner warms to *The R.M.* The appeal of the hunting life is there, but it is also a reminder of much that goes on in political Ireland. In his travels he will have met many a 'Flurry Knox' and a 'Roaring Jack'. And how could he fail to have a special sympathy for Major Sinclair Yeates, who left his regiment and England 'equipped with a feeling heart and the belief that two and two inevitably make four, whereas in Ireland two and two are just as likely to make five, or three, and are still more likely to make nothing at all.[1]

Indeed, if ever another pair of writing cousins emerge to write other 'Experiences', this time of 'An Irish Politician', it is certain that the adventures of Ulster's first Chief Minister would find their way into the account. The titles of the original tales would themselves make excellent chapter headings for the story: The Waters of Strife, A Conspiracy of Silence, Holy Island, The Policy of the Closed Door, or even, Sharper than a Ferret's Tooth.

Certainly there would be no shortage of local hearsay to fill the notebooks. In a relatively short political career, Faulkner has already become one of Ireland's most debated public figures. Small in stature, but larger than life, he has become a national talking-point, giving scope for all the subtle wit with which the Irish affectionately malign their politicians.

Where Brian Faulkner is concerned, Dr Johnson's remark about the Irish being 'a fair people' who 'never speak well of one another' is illustrated in full. It was apparent on his return from the Sunningdale Conference in December 1973 when he reported to the Northern Ireland Assembly on the new agreement. During that report he was interrupted incessantly and noisily and had to endure descriptions as varied as 'Lundy', 'King Rat' and 'the man who crawled out from under the stones'.[2] By any standard it was a marathon effort; it was a considerable demonstration of what R. A. Butler once called 'the patience of politics'.

Irish Faulkneralia is splendidly extravagant—cutting, yet at the same time containing a tang of admiration. Like the one commenting on the famous capacity to survive, whatever the hazard:

Question—'If Faulkner fell under a bus tomorrow, what on earth would happen?'

Answer—'The bloody bus would miss him!'

Other stories are more pugnacious and seek to bruise. Everyone knows, for instance, that Faulkner is Master of the local Hunt and a keen supporter. But this fact is often embellished by the 'inside information' that it is all a carefully arranged political recreation, designed to enhance voting appeal among the gentry of County Down.

Since Faulkner first rode to hunt at the age of eight, one can only conclude that he must have been a very far-sighted child.

Then, too, there is the famous 'secret property' deal, related and beloved from one end of Ireland to the other: 'Have you heard about the big estate he has bought in Scotland and the castle to go with it? Don't you see, he's getting ready for the day when Paisley throws him out. Shrewd fellow.'

Real life is less impressive and more parochial. As Faulkner himself puts it: 'Eight acres at Seaforde, Co. Down. That's my lot—not a rood more do I own.' But the talk continues; even the ten-roomed home which stands on the ground is authoritatively described in a local publication as 'a vast house in the country'.

When Faulkner himself is excused his father has often been

blamed. Even into his 'eighties the barbs continued. Irish political folk-lore insists that James Faulkner was the driving force all along—an Ulster version of Joseph Kennedy, manipulating his fortune to steer an obedient son to the political summit.

Brian Faulkner denies this and there is substance in the denial. No doubt his father was happy to see his son make progress and helped wherever possible, but James Faulkner always put the family business first in his consideration (even at the expense of removing his son from university in mid-course) and encouraged the business association to continue for some twenty years. Nor did Faulkner senior throw himself into Ulster party politics in order to prepare the way for a family influence. There are, indeed, a good many long-standing political families in the Province, but the Faulkners have been noted almost entirely for their industrial and commercial activities.

But the 'brooding father' image is firmly implanted. Even Terence O'Neill could not resist the temptation to allude to it. In a remarkable passage in his autobiography, the former Ulster Premier makes this comment about the ambitions of his rival: 'I didn't really blame Brian. I knew that the dominant power in the family was his father, who was desperately anxious to see his son as PM while he was still alive'.[3]

This digging for motive extends into every phase of family history. Not even schooling is overlooked. The liberal gesture of being boarded in a Dublin school is seen as a particularly Machiavellian touch: 'Didn't you know that Brian is something of a secret and fluent Gaelic speaker? It was drummed into him in Dublin—preparation for the day when he will be nominated as President of Ireland.'

In truth, this Northern 'all-rounder' is as notoriously illiterate in the native Irish as that most English and most popular of Irish Presidents, Erskine Childers, who now rules with such distinction from Phoenix Park, Dublin. Certainly, if one day Brian Faulkner should receive a Presidential nomination (and given the vagaries of Irish politics, it is not an impossible notion) it will not be because of his ability to converse with constituents in the western Gaelthact.

Such are the tales of mystery and imagination which surround Brian Faulkner. Everybody 'knows for certain' something about him—and it loses nothing in the telling. In fact, his private life has been one of withdrawal; he is something of a social recluse, very much in the public eye, but preferring his own company.

Nor does Faulkner bother much about improving his image. He insists (rather like Liam Cosgrave) on a very private sort of life, based on a jealously guarded family circle within the framework of the solid Ulster Presbyterian tradition which he supports. Even in normal times the Faulkners are rarely seen at popular public events; they belong to few societies and certainly there is no hectic social life beyond the home. When he does entertain he is a courteous host, but, again, within the strict personal habits of the considerable group of Ulster people who prefer a quiet family life and who neither smoke nor drink.

Indeed, until Faulkner became Prime Minister of Northern Ireland alcohol was never permitted into the household—its introduction was accepted as one of the burdens of high office. Even today the reluctance is evident—Brian Faulkner will offer his guest an Irish whiskey with all the enthusiasm of a Muslim waiter serving pork to a best friend.

Choice of recreations increase the tendency to isolation. Like Edward Heath, the Ulster leader is dedicated to personal fitness and enjoys his exercise at the local Hunt and in sailing. Beyond these activities there is little time or inclination to be more outgoing in personal relationships, particularly when there is plenty of opportunity to retire to the relaxing chores of country life.

Faulkner's self-reliance has sometimes been counter-productive. This has been especially evident during periods of acute personal crisis. Certainly when he has been under greatest pressure he has seemed at times very short of friends willing to spring to his defence. This was so during the most critical periods of his premiership and, in particular, during the five months of his first power-sharing executive.

Faulkner's reputation has also suffered by the timing of his rise to power. Following the O'Neill era, he had to suffer comparison with his predecessor among the world media. It was no easy task. O'Neill was a new type Unionist and a master of publicity, whose rise to power coincided with a developing period in the TV political programme. He recognised the opportunities inherent in the new situation and saw to it that his 'new frontier' policies became international news.

Also, for once, the Province had a prime minister who was politically photogenic: a descendant on one side of the ancient O'Neill clan and on the other from Sir Arthur Chichester, with Eton and the Guards as additional guarantees of pedigree. Enough to move even the staid *Economist* to remark on his 'impeccable lineage'.

O'Neill, in fact, was the dream of the public relations industry and he was given full and generous treatment. It was of little consequence that many Ulster people were less enthusiastic; in the eyes of his admirers O'Neill could do no wrong and those who thought otherwise ran the risk of being branded as backwoodsmen. When contradictions *did* appear they were ignored. An O'Neill who was a member of the Orange Order was regarded as a harmless manifestation of Irish eccentricity, while lesser men who held membership faced the charge of sectarianism. Even English radicals were prepared to ignore O'Neill's upper-class conservatism and his implacable opposition to the Labour movement—his virtual destruction of the Northern Ireland Labour Party in the 1965 Election proved a pyrrhic victory.

For the many who flocked to support this true son of the 'Big House' and the new Unionism he advocated so eloquently, his sudden resignation and departure for England was a traumatic experience; it was a 'Flight of the Earls' all over again, leaving them stunned and leaderless. They had no love for those who gained politically from his downfall or who seemed involved in that downfall. Many of these O'Neillites were among the most influential people in the Province; for a time their pursuit was unrelenting and damaging.

For Faulkner it was the fate of Lyndon Johnston all over again. The hand that killed John F. Kennedy may have been that of Lee Harvey Oswald, but it was the accession and the presence of L. B. J. that became the constant reminder of what had gone before.

So, too, with Faulkner. The final shattering blow which had forced O'Neill's resignation had been aimed at him by his cousin James Chichester-Clarke (though such is the complexity of Ulster politics that even this episode was regarded by many as a complicated 'Big House' move to retain control), but it was the coming of Faulkner that marked the real end of the O'Neill domination of Ulster politics.

That was the effective social revolution: the manufacturer's son was a vivid reminder that things would never again be the same in Northern Ireland.

Faulkner, like Johnston, did not find it easy to outdazzle the promise given by his forerunner nor to escape from policy constraints inherited from the past. Future American historians will, no doubt, give due weight to the legislative achievements and the civil rights advances under President Johnston, but present-day judgement is coloured by his handling of an inherited Vietnam war. Faulkner had similar problems: his premiership was overshadowed by security policies, partly his own and partly passed down from earlier generations of Unionist politicians.

But, unlike Johnston, the Unionist leader was young enough to start again and to learn from previous mistakes. Time and circumstances have been on his side and because he is working in a situation of unparalleled crisis his political skill is readily recognised.

This professional skill and dedication to the job—he is rich enough to retire to that imaginary Scottish country estate—is one of Faulkner's greatest assets, and more than any other Ulster politician of his generation he has employed his talents to build up a secure political base. Like another of Ulster's masters of tactics, Field Marshal Montgomery, he rarely moves into battle until he is sure that his forces are fully adequate and properly positioned.

When, for instance, he resigned as Leader of the Unionist Party he did so only after he had been appointed by the British Government as Chief Minister and had secured the loyalty of the key members of the headquarters staff. Some weeks earlier he had ordered the photostatting of all the party records (in case of bombing!) and had launched a rebuilding fund in his own name. When the break came, he was well prepared for the transfer.

Faulkner has also displayed an ability to come to terms with reality which, whatever the dangers, has enabled him to develop a changing strategy to meet the changing demands of the Irish political scene. This pragmatic approach has allowed him to enter into new alliances closed to his predecessors in office. Gerry Fitt, his deputy and life-long opponent, has recognised this ability and has paid tribute to his new leader and political ally for it: 'I personally believe that Brian Faulkner is the most realistic politician of his generation.'

This policy of pulling the party behind him may one day pay dividends, but in the short run it has set Faulkner at odds with many of his traditional supporters. As he put it when he was sworn in as Northern Ireland's new Chief Minister: 'I have given and taken many hard knocks in my day.' In recent years some of the knocks have fallen on the heads of former colleagues and friends; in the narrow confines of Ulster politics it has been an unsettling exercise.

More important, Faulkner's political base has been eroded as he has entered new alliances, forcing him to rely more and more on untested support. Throughout his career these twists and turns of policy have been recognised and accepted as part of his political style, but in more restless times sudden shifts in policy add to the uncertainty felt by the community.

At such moments an ability to communicate with the public becomes crucial. Should Faulkner ever forget this essential requirement he will lose his personal following and his own position with it. It is his greatest peril.

When faced with this criticism Ulster's Chief Minister will insist that commentators should weigh his words more carefully than they do. This is wise advice for he is a clever speaker, adept at dropping in the qualifying word or phrase which later becomes the basis of a whole new policy. He seems to recognise and positively enjoy the risk-taking involved in such tactics,

7

regarding the exercise as something of a personal challenge. As on the hunting field, he establishes his objective and pursues it with a finely controlled balance of nerve and judgement.

But politics is more than a hunt meeting and its spills are far more sudden and lasting in effect. Already this skilled politician has escaped a final fall by perilously close margins. What a failure his life would have seemed if the final judgement had been given when Stormont was closed by Edward Heath in 1972. Like many another politician he has been spared the embarrassment of having his reckoning taken at an inconvenient moment.

Here again, Faulkner the pragmatist interposes his own assessment. He will contend that risk-taking in specific situations is what political skill is all about. It is not a matter of luck; it is a matter of pursuing a policy within the limits of one's ability to exert control and knowing when the limit has been reached.

Arthur Brian Deane Faulkner has twenty-five turbulent years behind him to prove his capacity to survive. During that quarter century—co-terminous with the rise of the Northern Ireland state—he has become one of the most praised and pilloried public figures in Ireland. Often, too, the praise and the pillory have at different times come from precisely the same people and groups of organisations. With a fine impartiality, he has paid scant attention to all who probe his motives.

He would claim as Henry Fairlie did in *The Life of Politics* that public life 'demands that he should never try to seize imaginary initiatives or seek speedy results; that he should wait calmly for his opportunity; that he should never despair or panic. It demands that he should bear obloquy, misrepresentation and injuries without complaint; that he should expect no gratitude; that he should remain silent when one word would justify him, if that word would injure his cause.'[4]

And at the end of the day, Faulkner insists: 'Forget the theories and the preconceptions and judge me by what I have done.'

It is a fair challenge; it is the yardstick by which Ulster's first Chief Minister would measure those around him; and it is the rule by which he would wish his life so far to be assessed.

CHAPTER TWO

An Irish Preparation

The Faulkner family motto is *Fortuna Favente* (favoured by fortune). It is a good motto, but it does not tell the whole story; the family certainly have prospered since they came to serve the king in Ireland in the Middle Ages, but they have all shown a capacity for hard work which has enabled them to do well in trade and industry.

The family is mentioned in O'Hart's *Irish Pedigrees*, where it is recorded that Edmund Taylor of Beverley in Yorkshire, chief 'Falkener' to Henry III in 1273, was the ancestor of Taylor and Faulkner in Ireland.[5] Later references in Irish family genealogy confirm that the family came over from England and settled in the Dublin area, eventually spreading to many parts of the country. A branch of the connection was of some importance in County Longford in medieval times and others became known in Kerry, Mayo and in the Ulster Province where the usual spelling became 'Faulkner'.

By the seventeenth century Faulkners were numerous in Dublin, and of these George Faulkner was by far the most famous. George, born at the end of the seventeenth century, opened a printing business in Dublin in 1726 and made a small fortune through his famous *Dublin Journal*, and the publication of other works, said to be largely pirated. Like many printers of his day, George was also a man of affairs and used his business to subsidise many public activities.

He was a familiar figure in both London and Dublin society and became a confidant of many leading politicians including Lord Chesterfield, the Irish Viceroy. But it was in Dublin that he made his greatest mark, enjoying, as Dublin historian Maurice Craig puts it, 'a reputation and a social position which most poets would have envied, if envy were part of the make-up of poets'.[6]

George was a famous and hilarious host, departing wildly from the Presbyterian traditions of other branches of the family. On one occasion he had as guests at his dinner table a man who had been sentenced to death and reprieved as well as the judge who had presided at the trial. It is not recorded which enjoyed the reunion more, but George was certainly delighted with the occasion. He would also gaily tell stories to explain his possession of a wooden leg. The loss of the original, he claimed, had been the result of a frustrated love affair, a revengeful husband having interrupted it.

But this wholly delightful character has other claims to a place in the history of his time. He was a lifelong friend, printer and publisher to Jonathan Swift. He went out of his way to perform many services to the great and struggling author and did much to perpetuate Swift's reputation in Ireland after his death. George Faulkner's many public services were justly recognised when he was made a city Alderman in the later years of his life.

Another eighteenth-century Faulkner (Arthur Brooke) made a minor reputation as a writer of military history, but, in the main, most members of the family were content to concentrate on commerce.

A chance for the Northern Faulkners to expand their interests came with the industrial revolution. By the eighteenth century the textile industry was developing fast in Ireland and in the north the linen industry was beginning to attract energetic entrepreneurs. About the middle of the century Cookstown in County Tyrone was redesigned as a new growth centre by the local proprietor. Eighty-six miles from Dublin, Cookstown was already well established as a market and post town, and as the linen trade grew it became an important centre for bleaching, dyeing and finishing Irish linen for the English market.

It was in Cookstown that Brian Faulkner's forebears made their first mark on the commerce of Ulster. The family grew up in this pleasant and prosperous country town, described by a visitor in 1854 as sure to 'interest the visitor by the singularity of its appearance. It consists of a single street of great width, lined with trees on either side, combining the rusticity of an avenue with the sprightliness of a town and producing a very striking effect.' At the centre of the town was a large and handsome Presbyterian meeting house, the first minister of which won fame by his participation in the Siege of Londonderry. The Faulkners would have liked that.

Doyle also notes that early eighteenth-century Cookstown was 'a great market for the sale of raw linens and yarn and sums of money exchange hands upon the market days to an amount scarcely credible'.[7]

It was in this bustling North Irish setting that Brian Faulkner's grandparents founded a flax mill, confidently expecting to make the fortune which would provide for the upkeep of their fine home and seven children. For some years the business flourished, but the rot set in when grandfather Faulkner took to drink and from that time till his death the family fortunes went into a rapid and disastrous decline.

Left on her own, grandmother Faulkner with typical Victorian pride and energy sold her possessions and moved the family to Belfast, where she established herself in a modest house in the east of the city. Here in Templemore Avenue, within sight of the local shipyards, she continued her work as a teacher and encouraged her family to lay the foundations for sound academic and business careers. Grannie Faulkner became a much loved figure in this famous working-class district and lived on within sight of the shipyards until her death in 1940.

Young Brian Faulkner was deeply influenced by his grandmother and through her received an insight into the working-class areas of the capital city, which might have been impossible to gain from his country base. He retains to this day a great affection and respect for the qualities of his paternal grandmother.

James Faulkner (father of Brian) was the youngest son. He was sent to the Belfast Model School, renowned for its high standards and hard work. Here he received an excellent basic education which prepared him for the life of sturdy independence which his mother urged him to pursue. He also learned from his mother the virtues of thrift which ultimately made him an outstanding chairman of the Ulster Savings Movement.

One other lesson James had learned from bitter experience was 'don't drink', and in his private life he became a firm advocate of the temperance cause. To help his young family appreciate his argument, he offered £100 as a twenty-first birthday present if by then total abstinence had been maintained. Brian qualified for the reward. In this respect the story is told of Harold Wilson offering Faulkner a drink. When refusal was accompanied by the £100 story, Harold, quick as a flash, remarked: 'Ah, I see. I suppose you are now earning your second hundred.' Brian's reply is not recorded.

James Faulkner, on finishing his schooling in Belfast, decided to return to Cookstown where he entered the local linen trade, rapidly building up for himself a reputation as a sales representative in the north of England. Through his efforts the local firm prospered and before long young James began to wonder whether he might not do better on his own account.

It is said that his mind was finally made up when one evening, after a particularly successful selling tour in England, he was called to the manager's office and, with considerable ceremony, presented with a sealed envelope 'in recognition of your services'. On returning to his lodgings he discovered that the reward consisted of one gold sovereign; he decided to seek his own recognition and soon set off for Belfast, Northern capital and centre of the Irish linen industry, where he knew that his talents would find a ready outlet.

Fortunately for James Faulkner, at that time he met Andrew Latimer, who like himself was a linen man through and through. Combining their meagre capital, these two in the years following the First World War began to manufacture semi-stiff collars, for which there was a ready market. It was, as one operative who knew them puts it, 'a true knife and fork' affair, and developed into one of Ireland's most important shirt factories. They started in a small room, but a flourishing joint family business grew, and there was a time when they occupied a building which later became headquarters for the Unionist Party. Eventually they combined the first three letters of their surnames to produce a world-famous trade mark of

'Faulat'—the Irish shirt with the patent magic reversible cuff.

To this day the family talk proudly of their product. Even Brian Faulkner, not given to nostalgia, still remembers with pride the family commercial activity and the finished article. There is also pride in price: 'A shirt and three collars for 6/11 in 1939—how's that for value?'. How, indeed—a reminder of different times in Ulster, as elsewhere.

This family factory business was to play a formative influence in the life of young Brian Faulkner. It provided him with a 'grass roots' knowledge of an industry which, as much as ships, was part of the essential Ulster. It provided, too, the basis of the Faulkner family fortune so that a political career could be pursued without regard to the financial hazards which accompany a full-time political career in the limited prospects offered by Northern Ireland. But in the 1920s, when James Faulkner was establishing the family business, such considerations were still far ahead for his eldest son.

Brian Faulkner was born at Helen's Bay, a pleasant seaside area in Co. Down on 18 February 1921. He was christened Arthur Brian Deane. Brian was selected 'because the family liked it' and Arthur Deane came from his mother's side. Since his birth, the family has remained in Co. Down and the links with this pleasant county go deep. He still lives in the county at Seaforde and can think of no other place he would rather live. No other Ulster leader has deeper or more permanant roots; he also retains close links with his mother and is a very frequent visitor to her home in Cultra.

Faulkner's early childhood was spent in a series of farm homes, each reflecting the growing prosperity of the family, where, along with his younger brother Denis, he acquired a working knowledge of Ulster country life. By any standard it was a comfortable childhood, and the family grew up in material comfort denied to many in Ulster between the wars. They had the benefit of a series of good schools, though with four before the age of 14, there was little opportunity to settle into any of them. Because of this, Faulkner never had much opportunity to make lifelong local friendships at school, a factor which accentuated his natural introvert tendencies.

Eventually in 1935 James Faulkner decided to prepare his son for university entrance by entering him at St Colomba's College, Rathfarnham, a famous Irish public school outside Dublin. The fees were high by Irish standards, but James Faulkner was prepared to pay the price to get the right article.

St Columba's was founded in 1843 by the Lord Primate, Lord Dunraven, William Sewell (subsequently founder of Radley) and others for the education of the sons of members of the Church of England and of Ireland. The college was incorporated by Royal Charter in 1913 and retains its reputation as one of Ireland's most select colleges. All in all, and particularly in view of its Anglican tradition, it was an odd choice for a Northern Presbyterian father.

James Faulkner argued that for anyone who was to live and work in the North a period of education in the southern capital would have a beneficial and broadening effect. He felt sure, too, that his son would be able to resist any proselytising influence. He was right. Early in his school career Brian was informed by the Headmaster that all the senior pupils were to be confirmed by the Lord Archbishop of Dublin and that he was to make himself available for the appropriate ceremonies. Young Faulkner immediately let the Headmaster know in no uncertain terms that he was a Northern Presbyterian and would remain so, no matter what the school tradition might be. There was no confirmation; he still feels proud of this act of defiance on behalf of Presbyterianism.

At school Brian formed a close friendship with Michael Yeats, son of the Irish poet, W. B. Yeats. Though they were of the same age and arrived at and went through the school together, they were an oddly contrasting pair—the huge Michael, an out-and-out Republican, and the smallish Northerner, with his solid Presbyterian-Unionist background. But they were ideal companions and the views and comments on Irish life that each brought to the relationship were different from any either of the boys had known before. Both, on leaving school, gravitated towards politics; Michael became a well-known barrister and a prominent member of the Fianna Fail Party and Speaker of the Dublin Senate.

With young Yeats, Faulkner threw himself into his new life at St Columba's and quickly adjusted to the atmosphere of a Dublin school. He became editor of the school magazine, and English Studies and the debating society formed the core of his school activities. Stimulated by the friendly opposition of young Yeats, he became more aware of his own background and learned to relate it to the total scene. He remained a staunch Ulster Unionist—but an Irish dimension was added which has never vanished. On one occasion in debate he proposed the motion: 'Ulster will fight and Ulster will be right'—stirrings of things to come! But more often than not, he and Michael Yeats combined their considerable debating skills to oppose the motion whatever the wording.

Faulkner retains happy memories of his days at St Columba's and regards Dr Willis, his housemaster, as having been one of the great influences of his life; but time and political distance have lessened the contact and except for Yeats few of his schoolboy links remain. A family connection with the college was broken when his own sons were sent to Glenalmond in Perthshire, though that college, too, has links with the Dublin establishment.

While at St Columba's, Faulkner was given little opportunity to get to know the nearby southern capital. Dublin, however, was famous horse country and young Faulkner was able to continue and develop his great interest in this popular Irish activity. The Faulkner family's love of horses is deep and long standing; it is very much in keeping with the Irish way of life. Riding and racing may be the sport of kings in other lands, but in Ireland, both North and South, the ordinary people are close to their animals and most Irish farmers take pride in breeding and riding good horses. As one expert has put it: 'No country in the world is better suited for raising horses and no people more intelligent in breeding them than the Irish.'[8]

James Faulkner, country born, grew up with a great love for horses. In his early days he was too poor to have a mount of his own, but as a young boy in Belfast he was a willing part-time groom on the local polo grounds, earning his rides by brushing down the horses of the Ulster gentry. Early in his marriage one of his first luxuries was the purchase of a horse. Since then the Faulkner family have always owned a small stable.

The love of horses is, in fact, a father-to-son tradition and today Brian Faulkner owns six horses, all members of his family sharing in their use. Horses have had a great influence in the life style of this Ulster politician. Even his home reflects this interest. Instead of a book-lined study, the sitting-room is lined with sporting prints; hunting apparatus and trophies are scattered around. And when Faulkner talks about his sport a fresh and relaxed side of him appears: enthusiasm and warmth enter into the presentation. Horses he certainly likes, but his real love is for the hunt. He talks of 'the music' of the hunt; the way in which a good master 'can control the pack as though it were an obedient and well controlled orchestra'. For a moment you can almost hear the thunder of the horses through the room. It is like having Neville Cardus describe a fine stroke in cricket or using imagery to record the flight of a ball sent down by one of his favourites; or listening to John Betjeman extol the virtues of a Victorian railway station.

Faulkner's philosophy of hunting goes deep. He has little time for riding as such. It is the pursuit itself that matters, 'the challenge to find the quarry and then to capture it'. This, for Faulkner, is the real thrill and it is one which he claims few people appreciate fully.

This love of blood sports and Faulkner's defence of it has put him 'off side' with liberals on many occasions and his opponents have not been slow to take advantage of his dedication. For a time in the old Stormont a favourite Labour ruse was to put questions down to the Minister of Commerce for answer on Wednesday afternoon, knowing full well that the Minister liked to be with his horses on that day. This was one Labour sport that was not appreciated by the member for East Down! More surprisingly, Faulkner's aristocratic rivals in the Unionist Party have not hesitated to use his love of the hunt against him. One suspects that they were not worried about the quarry but were more anxious to suggest that the hunter was 'getting above his station'.

But Faulkner's love of hunting is genuine and as Master and

Huntsman of the Co. Down Iveagh Hunt he turns out most Saturdays, October to March, from 12.00 to 4.30 p.m. and when possible on Wednesdays as well.

Faulkner's interest in hunting has also brought him social contacts which have proved valuable politically. His public image has often been one of caution where the Southern Irish are concerned but where horses and hunting combine he has never allowed politics to intervene. Down the years he has been a regular visitor to the Dublin Horse Show and long before North/South meetings were formalised he had got to know leading politicians in the Republic through these occasions. Liam Cosgrave shares his passion for hunting; it gives them an interest in common in a land where matters of mutual concern between North and South are all too rarely explored.

It was also at a hunting occasion in 1948 that Faulkner met his future wife, Lucy Forsythe, daughter of a well-known Bangor family. Combining good looks with a sharp and lively intelligence (kept all the sharper by journalism for the *Belfast Telegraph* and later as secretary to Lord Brookeborough), she was ideally fitted for the arduous political partnership which lay ahead. When they married in 1951 she could not realise how arduous the political trials would be, but fortunately she has been able to take the spills of the hustings as well as of the hunt, and throughout the intervening years she has been the determined centre of the family circle and a constant companion when the political going has been roughest.

At such moments she has not hesitated to enter into the fray on her husband's behalf. Lucy Faulkner has a firm grasp of the grim realities of Ulster politics. She has been discreet in her interventions, but when necessary can express herself with pointed clarity. Recent evidence of this appeared in *The Times*, when in a rare letter she gently but convincingly reminded Professor John Vaizey of what hardship really means to those who live under the threat of constant terror. Vaizey in a frank letter had expressed his opinion, common enough among intellectuals in Britain, that the time had come for London 'to withdraw and for Dublin to assume its responsibilities and for Dublin to choose'.

Vaizey who wrote from the very different world of Kippford in Kirkcudbrightshire must have been surprised at the strength of the rebuff he received:

LETTER TO THE TIMES, 24 August 1973

FUTURE OF NORTHERN IRELAND

From Mrs Brian Faulkner

Sir, Living as he does in the delightful and serene village of Kippford on the Urr—generations of my family have been lying peacefully on the other side of the river for some 300 years—I can understand Professor Vaizey's direct and intellectual approach to the problems of Northern Ireland, and the distaste for us all which he obviously feels (August 23).

But may I ask him to temper his cool verdict with humanity and justice.

It should not be necessary to explain to Professor Vaizey the conditions under which ordinary people are living here. We, too, have retreats in Ulster like Kippford where death and mutilation and the crumph of bombs seem as unreal as they are to him, but we know also that if his "solution" were adopted, even those shelters of comparative peace would disappear overnight and not any of us—Unionist or Republican, Protestant or Catholic—would find a bolthole from the holocaust that would follow.

Blood is being shed today, as Professor Vaizey rightly says: in three years, 800 deaths from violence. Would he still rest quietly in his bed by the Urr if it were ten times that in three months?

The ease with which the small number of sadistic fanatics can destroy a community has been a frightening revelation to us all in Northern Ireland. Candidates of militant organizations took only 3 per cent of the poll in the elections for the new Assembly.

"The British", writes Professor Vaizey, "have no strong reason to remain (in Northern Ireland)". Northern Ireland has been part of the United Kingdom since 1800, and continued as such after the citizens of the Irish Republic opted out some 50 years ago. At the border referendum in March this year, 66 per cent of the population voted to remain British. Statistics proved that between 15 and 20 per cent of those votes were cast by members of the religious minority, traditionally considered to be Republicans. Have all these British citizens now "no strong reason to remain" here?

We envy the people who live by the Urr. We want to return to a way of life where "peace" means the sound of the sea and the seagulls and not, as it does for all of us at the moment, the end of the war against the IRA.

Yours faithfully,
LUCY FAULKNER,
Seaforde,
Downpatrick.

Few letters to *The Times* have spelt out so eloquently the passion of the Ulster crisis and the special strain endured by the women of the politicians involved.

When Faulkner married in 1951 he settled down in the village of Spa in County Down and remained there until 1960 when he moved to his present home at Seaforde, still in the same county. During these years he had been combining business with politics and it is this period he looked back on as one of the most satisfying of his life. He is particularly proud of his work as an industrialist, something which he stresses as 'an essential part of my life'.

Industrial life was thrust upon Faulkner abruptly, but such was his family loyalty that he accepted the change without question. He had left St Columba's in 1939 and entered Queen's University as a law student. He commenced his studies under the formidable Professor Montrose, one of Northern Ireland's outstanding and radical educationists, and looked forward to the usual three or four years of academic life. He had no great desire to take up law as a career but it was generally agreed that it 'would be useful in business'. Then, too, there was the uncertainty of war, and he prepared for this event by enlisting in the O.T.C.

But a sudden crisis in the Faulkner business changed the plans of the whole family. Due to the departure on war service of some key members of staff the firm ran into a serious man-power crisis. The family firm was in danger and the Faulkners were expected to rally to its aid. It was indicated to the eldest son that his duty was to the firm and that he should make himself available. In 1940 he left Queen's University and his legal career and for the next five years concentrated on gearing the firm to war work and on carrying through a modernisation programme to speed up production.

Instead of serving as an officer in the regular forces he had to serve in the LDV and the Home Guard attached to the firm. Faulkner never regretted this decision and became closely identified with Ulster's industrial war effort; under his management the firm prospered and with it the family fortune. By the end of the war the undertaking had doubled in size and a greatly strengthened and diversified business had been built up.

Not all of Faulkner's ideas were popular with the workers or the trade unions and neither he nor his father took easily to what they regarded as interference in managerial affairs. Joint consultation and industrial democracy have never won ready acceptance in the ranks of Ulster-born management. Indeed, until he won a reputation as a 'job getter' for the Province, Faulkner was regarded with considerable coolness by the trade union movement. However, the firm were fair employers and in a period when wage cutting was the order of the day the workers were paid above the Trade Board rates.

Miss Sadie Patterson, MBE, veteran Irish trade union leader, still remembers her tussles with the Faulkners and their resistance to trade union influences. Of James Faulkner she says: 'He was a hard nut to crack, but there was a softness there if you could get through'. One example of this softness is remembered in trade union circles as regards the sister of a leading trade unionist who had been blacklisted in the clothing trade because of her family connections. When she applied to Faulkner's firm she was taken on and stayed with them for many years. Faulkner commented at the time: 'Her family background is no concern of mine. She is a good worker and deserves the job.'

Brian Faulkner set about preparing the company for the post-war market and went on a series of promotional tours which gave the firm an impressive share of overseas trade and the young promoter an equally impressive knowledge of markets in Europe and America which eventually he was able to put to good use in government service.

Faulkner stayed with his firm until 1960 when he became a government minister. Three years later the thriving business was merged with the Ladybird group, and the Faulkner family sold out their controlling interest.

But already in 1945 Faulkner was beginning to feel the urge to seek a challenge beyond industry. He was still deeply interested in the firm and continued to serve it for another 15 years, but he was attracted by the political arguments of his day concerning the future of his Province. His years in Dublin had made him more aware of his Northern heritage and of the need to express it in terms appropriate to the post-war world. He had already noted the growing impact of the trade union and Labour movement on the Province and the way in which Labour candidates were winning seats. Pre-war Unionism, he decided, would be no answer to post-war socialism.

But in the aftermath of war few listened to the young Unionist from Co. Down who was becoming interested in politics. Neither he nor his family carried much weight in the inner circles of Unionism and there were others with more charisma about. Admittedly he had done his bit as an industrialist during the war, but in a Province where there are more Captains and Majors to the political square mile than at Sandhurst, he lacked the glamour of war service. For such as he, nomination was not available in 1945—he would have to wait.

But even then Faulkner had mastered 'the patience of politics'. In the years to come he would illustrate R. A. Butler's (a man he admires) vivid phrase on more than one occasion; in the meantime he was prepared to wait and to prepare the ground carefully for the political career which he sensed now awaited him.

As Unionist seats toppled to Labour in Belfast he was more than ever convinced that the ideas he brought could revive the Ulster Unionist Party; all he needed was a base from which to propound his plans and make himself known. In 1946 he found that base.

CHAPTER THREE

Orange and Protestant Way

Brian Faulkner's entry into politics bears all the marks of the careful planning which has distinguished each phase of his career. He examined the possibilities carefully, waiting patiently for an opportune moment, then moved decisively. Rarely in terms of his objective has he made a mistake; rarely, too, has he been willing to admit making one.

The family could provide no ready-made power base, for though his father, James Faulkner, had signed the Covenant and taken out Unionist Party membership he had never taken a leading part in the control of the movement. There were, however, inherited advantages and, in particular, the firm connection with the powerful Presbyterian Church was important.

Religion and politics (less so, Christianity and politics) are closely interwoven in Ireland, and though it would be an oversimplification to suggest that the conflict in Northern Ireland is a 'Holy War', religion remains a factor of great importance in public life and debate. Deep down, of course, the confrontation has more to do with politics and economics than anything else; indeed, if all Ireland were to become non-Christian tomorrow the basic political arguments would remain, for many of the most committed leaders care little for religion and some of them are bitterly opposed to all branches of the Church. However, it is still the practice in Northern Ireland for political issues to be expressed in denominational terms and so the Church connection remains a matter of great importance. 'Consciousness of kind' has been encouraged at every level of society and is reflected in all activity whether at work or school or play.

In these circumstances, it has been the traditional practice of 'Orange' and 'Green' establishment politicians to make their point through sectarian institutions and in the language of one or other religious grouping. Since nearly everyone is 'churched' from the moment of birth (and in Ireland even the atheist knows his Church!) it has been the custom in the North for political parties to encourage sectarian voting patterns— Protestants, in general, voting for one or other brand of Unionism, and Catholics supporting Nationalist/Republican groups. So politics have taken on a horizontal divide. Few of those wishing to get on in politics have been able to resist the pull of the main sectarian groups, so, consequently, there has been a good deal of cross-fertilisation between Church and party political membership. Political priests abound and all too often the pulpit becomes a spiritual husting for the appointed of the Party.

In recent years (and more so in the past decade) the Churches have been making an effort to weaken their involvement with party politics and have been searching out new forms of inter-Church co-operation. But in the 1940s, when Faulkner decided to enter politics, inter-Church relationships were not greatly encouraged in Ireland and ecumenism was regarded by many people in Northern Ireland as a subtle word inserted into the vocabulary of religion at the special instigation of the Vatican.

Even at the beginning of his career Faulkner did not need to be reminded of such things; he had grown up in a solid Unionist home and he understood the facts of local political life. Fortunately with organised religion he was in good standing and, as a Presbyterian, belonged to the largest denomination in Northern Ireland, with some 400,000 members. He is and always has been a loyal supporter of his local church and pays tribute to the influence which his minister and others he has known have had on his life. However, contrary to the popular view of him as a rigid Bible Presbyterian, there is not much evidence that he is unduly worried about or even well-up in the finer points of theology. He turns up occasionally as a visitor to the General Assembly of the Presbyterian Church, but has never been prominent in Church debates. Now and again he has played to the crowd by taking a dutiful swing at the World Council of Churches and on one occasion even at *The Song of Bernadette* (the real one, not Miss Devlin), but deep down it is unlikely that he concerns himself much about doctrine. Equally, he is not likely to risk the loss of votes by sponsoring Church unity moves.

But in the 1940s Faulkner was a young man in search of a platform. Having missed war service, he needed an interest with which he could identify. For a Unionist what could be better than a Protestant defender and where better to pursue such a course than through membership of the Loyal Orange Institution of Ireland? In addition, the stimulating debates at his Dublin school had awakened in him a genuine interest in the Protestant tradition. The Order, he felt, could give him the outlet he sought. The decision to join the Orange Order was at the same time a gesture of independence; his family were surprised at the move and his involvement with the Order has remained a very personal affair throughout his career.

Since its establishment in 1795 the Orange Order has been an essential part of the North Irish political scene and since the creation of the state its influence on and through the Unionist Party has been crucial. Unionists claim that the relationship is similar to that of the trade unions with the Labour Party— with separate yet overlapping memberships giving opportunities to wield influence. They overlook, however, the sectarian and communally divisive effects of the more extreme forms of Orangeism.

The Orange Order now has branches throughout the Commonwealth and the USA and remains a stout defender of the Protestant faith. But Orangeism is more than a religious organisation. In Northern Ireland its influence has been enormous and its ranks provided an umbrella under which a remarkable triple alliance of the landed aristocracy, the *nouveau riche* and the working classes was achieved in the nineteenth and twentieth centuries. This vast inter-class alliance worked to the advantage of the substantial group of landed aristocrats and businessmen who held key posts in the Order. These members, because of their superior wealth and organising ability, were able, through the Order, to extend their political influence into working-class areas of society normally reserved for radical movements. Even the Protestant trade unionists were staunchly Orange and were persuaded to support a political policy often opposed to trade union aims.

In fact, Orange power and political power have gone hand in hand in Northern Ireland. Inevitably, too, a Protestant emphasis was given to politicians who joined the Order; and, equally inevitably, they became associated with confessional politics and estranged from their Roman Catholic constituents. It could hardly be otherwise. As one official historian of the Order has put it: 'Orangeism is a philosophy of life for many people in Northern Ireland. It is much more than membership of the organisation known legally as "The Loyal Orange Institution of Ireland". It is a way of life, a way of looking at religion, politics, morality and charity. It is not just Protestantism or Unionism or even a bit of both. It is the conviction that Reformed Christianity is the Faith by which to live and that the theological motivation should regulate the thoughts, words and actions of everyone who subscribes to it.

Anyone who sees Orangeism as anything other than or less than this has failed to understand what it is all about.'[9]

Non-members of the Orange Order (Protestant as well as Catholic) have not contested the right of such a group to promote a specific religious viewpoint or to engage in the voluntary service activities (many of them of a charitable and social nature) of the Order; it is the political link that has caused concern.

And here the position is clear: 'The Orange Institution has never tried to hide its involvement with the Ulster Unionist Party which it brought into birth in the early days of the Home Rule controversy.'[10]

It is, of course, claimed that the Institution does not manipulate the Party, but with representation at constituency associations and central executive levels the influence of the Order penetrates deep into every decision-making structure. Few

Unionist politicians have failed to play the 'Orange card' when required; some may have been embarrassed by the ritual, but it is still true that on the great Twelfth of July annual marches to celebrate the 1690 Battle of the Boyne victory of the Protestant King William III over Roman Catholic James II even the most reluctant politician member of the Order dusts his Sash and marches with the local demonstration to display his loyalty in speech and song.

Since 1969 there has been growing criticism of the Orange/Unionist link; with the growing fragmentation of Unionism it is likely that the connection will weaken. But in 1946 when Faulkner joined the Orange Order such criticism, if voiced at all in government circles, was muted and it was the done thing for ambitious Unionists to don the Sash. Whatever their conflicting views on party policy, Ulster's top Tories all met at the Lodge. People as diverse in outlook as Terence O'Neill and William Craig have been brethren together. Equally, someone as urbane and independent in thought as Phelim O'Neill remained a member until he was expelled for the ecumenical gesture of attending a Roman Catholic service; even someone as politically debonair as Roy Bradford has felt unable to resist the call of the Sash. So, in joining the Order, Faulkner was doing nothing unusual.

Getting into a Lodge was no problem for the new recruit. His father had no membership but he had plenty of influential Orange contacts. Arrangements were made for his son to be received into the well-known Eldon Lodge in Belfast, two local notables, Sir Herbert Dixon and Tom Somerset, MP acting as sponsors. Some regarded the choice of Lodge as rather exclusive ('one that seldom sits and never walks'), but the new member proved to be much more than a nominal supporter of this and every other loyalist organisation with which he formed an association.

Faulkner differed from most of his party contemporaries in the extent to which he identified with the Order. He was no mere 'Twelfth Day' man—the Orange Institution was for him a way of life and a structure through which he reached a wider section of Ulster life. Through the Order with its 100,000 members he was able to make contact with every level of social life in the Province, so making up in some way for the opportunities lost during his out-of-Ulster schooldays.

At no time in his career has Faulkner sought to qualify his Orange obligations nor has he considered them incompatible with his public duties. He has been much more than a fair-weather friend of the Order and even when his policies have been opposed he has continued his support. When, for instance, his leadership was rejected, partly by Orange votes, at the Unionist Council meeting in January 1974, he reaffirmed his position: 'I am a member of the Orange Order—a keen, enthusiastic member—and intend to remain.' He also claimed at the same time that the Orange Order was 'one of the most democratic institutions in the world'.

In a sense, of course, he is hoist by his own petard. Down the years he has defended the political link with the Order and has resisted the view that the link ought to be severed. He has not agreed (though it is unlikely that his new Unionist organisation will seek a formal link with the Institution) with those who wish to see the Order as a solely religious organisation. He has turned to the theme on many occasions.

In a typical reply to critics, he concluded: 'I do not doubt the sincerity of those who say that the Orange Order is entirely religious and not political. But I say with equal sincerity that they are not only misguided but hopelessly wrong. If we want to confine the Order purely to religion and divorce it from politics, then we must accept the fact that we will weaken its influence and deprive it of the opportunity of giving leadership in this country.' [11] All very much what the official historians of the Orange Institution believe.

This speech was typical of many made at Orange gatherings in his pre-Cabinet days and at no time did he seem to regard his Party's identification with one brand of religion in a divided community as a permanent impediment standing in the way of communal unity. Like most main-stream politicians, Unionist and Nationalist alike, he took the divide as something that had to be accepted: 'The situation in Ireland is such that politics and religion are completely interwoven. You cannot separate the one from the other.' It was a short-sighted view of politics that led straight to 'tribal' assumptions.

In fairness to Faulkner, before the concept of power sharing was explored, the two-nation theory was generally accepted in Northern Ireland and he was merely spelling out in public what most of his political contemporaries practised and believed. But it was his total alignment with the Orange Order that marked him out for special notice, earning for him among Protestants a 'true Blue' reputation. He did not object to such a reputation, though he did object to suggestions that he was at the same time anti-Catholic.

He paid a heavy price for such obtuseness. His Orange activities in the fifties and sixties often involved him in hawkish Protestant positions. On one occasion in 1955 he led a procession with bands and banners flying into Catholic country down a (ever after famous) lane near Kilkeel, in Co. Down, known as the Longstone Road. Flanked by a formidable RUC escort, he and his friends made their way, giving great offence to the Catholic community and involving the police in an embarrassing confrontation.

In vain did he subsequently plead in the Commons that he was only establishing that 'a band or procession lawfully marching or parading in Northern Ireland will be free to fly the Union Jack when on a public road. The Union Jack is the flag of this country and is entitled to be carried along our public highways'.

This strictly legalistic view was typical of Faulkner's response to accusations by his opponents that he was one-sided in his interpretation over what constituted freedom of movement. For many years he disputed the widely held view that incidents such as the Longstone Road and controversial marches in Londonderry City were likely to cause communal tension.

Even when he became Minister of Home Affairs in 1959 he was reluctant to take a firm line with marches likely to cause sectarian strife. Again he preferred to hide behind a legal formula: 'Might I make it absolutely clear that this Government are quite fit to govern and see that there is true civil and religious liberty. By that term I mean civil and religious liberty for all the people of Northern Ireland. If the police can convince me that there is going to be a breach of the peace in any part of Northern Ireland I will not hesitate to give them my absolute support.'

However, he took some convincing. Indeed, not until he became Prime Minister in 1971 was he persuaded that it was necessary to curtail the marching activities of his own supporters. By then he was a wiser man and he did, in fact, rule firmly against both Protestant and Catholic processions. (Ironically, action against one such group, 'The Apprentice Boys of Derry', led to his expulsion from that exclusive Protestant organisation.)

But 1971 was late in the day to establish a reputation as a mediator between Ulster's two communities; the success sought and won in the formative part of his career as an Orangeman meant inevitably a corresponding degree of alienation from the Roman Catholic community. It was a heavy price to pay for Party support; it meant that any future liberal policies he might proclaim would be judged against a background of suspicion based on bitter memories. And, as the saying goes, 'Ireland is a country that never forgets'.

But is the record one of total opposition to things Catholic?

To all charges of being anti-Catholic Faulkner points repeatedly to the full range of facts which constitute his behaviour. He will argue: 'Being pro-Protestant does not mean that one is anti-Catholic.' Again comes the demand: 'Judge me on what I have done.' He claims emphatically that his practical contributions to the community have been essentially ecumenical in tone and compare favourably with those of his colleagues and opponents.

It is in the field of industry that his ability to cross the religious divide has been most marked. Here the record is impressive and there is plenty of evidence of practical involvement with Roman Catholics at all levels. As trade union leaders testify, he has a good non-sectarian record in a city where 'employ your own' has too often been the unfortunate rule. He was also the first Unionist leader to introduce laws forbidding religious discrimination in public sector employment and he has encouraged an extension of the protection into the private sector as well.

Nor has Faulkner ever belonged to that narrow-minded group who would have nothing to do with the South. He knows the Republic well (his enemies say too well) and has close links, both personal and business. When young, the family holidays were spent caravanning in the west of Ireland, with Achill Island a favourite spot (it was on one of these outings in the 1950s that he first met Liam Cosgrave), and, of course, the Dublin Horse Show was for many years an annual event. In trade and industry links with the South Faulkner has been an emphatic supporter. Unlike other more shrill Protestant leaders he has resisted any attempt to mix politics with industry and, more than any other Unionist leader, has explored North-South trade possibilities. On tourism, for example, he has advocated Belfast/Dublin co-operation and sees no reason why a one-island view of the subject should not be taken. The border is there, but he recognises that in the eyes of most tourists it is non-existent. As he has put it: 'I am very hopeful that this is one sector of the economy in which we can co-operate with the South for the benefit of both parts of Ireland, because the average tourist, especially the one who comes from across the Atlantic is concerned more with the geography than with the political nature of the country he is visiting.' [12] This is a fair sample of his thinking on North/South economic relations and in many respects he has been ahead of Southern politicians on the subject.

In fact, as far as Faulkner is concerned, the border has little commercial relevance; with him, trade knows no political theology. As a private industrialist he has been willing to do business with the South and as a politician he has stressed repeatedly that he would be delighted 'to welcome any industrialist from the 26-counties who was prepared to provide employment in Northern Ireland'. He dismisses emphatically the views of those who would wage economic war against the South and, as Minister of Commerce, was at pains to stress that there was nothing at variance with the upholding of Unionist principles and taking part in discussions about lowering tariffs between the two parts of Ireland. In recent years he has encouraged industrial contacts between Belfast and Dublin and as his influence has grown so too has economic contact between the two states. He is particularly proud of the joint machinery which exists to secure economic co-operation. He is also a firm supporter of involvement through the EEC and talks of the opportunities provided by joint membership of the Community. He has been very quick to recognise the economic implication for Ireland as a whole and believes that the Market will give Ulster and the rest of Ireland a significant European dimension.

The most important manifestation of Faulkner's non-sectarian approach to industry in recent years has come in his opposition to those who suggest that industrial action should be used to pursue political ends. Such action would inevitably involve sectarian conflict among workers and would be a particularly harmful source of strife. In his opposition to political strikes he has had to face Protestant leaders like William Craig and organisations like the Loyalist Association of Workers, who together have urged the use of the strike weapon as a means of bringing pressure to bear upon government policies. Faulkner, with the support of the official trade union movement and the employers, has resisted such calls and in the constitutional crises of 1972 and 1974 was adamant in his opposition. Instinctively he senses that an introduction of religious strife to the factory floor would destroy the fabric of Ulster industry which he has endeavoured to build up during his most rewarding years in politics. Political strife in industry is for him the ultimate sectarian folly; he has not hesitated to describe it as such. In this attitude he has won support from both sides of industry.

Additional evidence of Faulkner's willingness to cross the sectarian divide came in October 1971 when he approached Dr G. B. Newe, one of Ireland's most prominent Roman Catholic laymen, to become a member of his government. Here, again, a tradition was being broken and, significantly, it was being changed by the most Orange of all the prime ministers of Northern Ireland. For both Newe and Faulkner the experiment was both unique and historic, but it went well. The public accepted the situation and the introduction of a Catholic into the cabinet room at Stormont was achieved without great fuss. During and since his term of office Ulster's first Catholic member of a Unionist government has paid tribute to Faulkner's personal qualities and to the way in which the team was led. As Dr Newe put it when his term of office ended: 'During my time in office I discovered a remarkable desire on the part of those in government to build a new society. Never did I hear any talk of sectarianism or Orangeism.' This was a generous tribute from a noted Ulster Catholic.

But unfortunately for Faulkner such tributes from Catholics down the years have been all too few. His political life-style has not encouraged points of contacts with leaders of Catholic religious and political opinion and inevitably he has been judged through the filter of his Orange activities. Only when he became prime minister did he begin to probe the Catholic community, but by then it was late in the day. Catholic judgement has therefore been harsh where Faulkner has been concerned.

Yet it could hardly be otherwise. In the early phases of his career his Orange membership earned him a reputation as a 'hard-liner' and most Catholics came to know him through his more extravagant speeches and gestures. It is certainly true, as he argues, that as an active spokesman of the Orange he was vulnerable to criticism because, unlike many of his colleagues who were nominal members of the Order, he used the annual rallies as an opportunity to enter into dialogue with the Unionist rank and file. Many of his more positive contributions on these occasions undoubtedly got less attention than those comments which touched on raw political nerves.

But such a defence is not enough. On these occasions he was speaking to the whole Province and he must have known it. The more heady stuff may have been directed at the faithful, but it also had a wider audience. Among Catholics it produced a sense of alienation—and such a gulf between Protestant and Catholic was, after all, what the Ulster problem was all about. Faulkner undoubtedly contributed to the widening of that gulf in some of his most active Orange years; it is hard to believe that someone as politically aware as he did not realise the implication of what he was doing. Statesmanship demands superior standards. It was no use arguing that, Unionist and

Nationalist alike, leading politicians of the day followed a similar course.

More tragically, Faulkner's superb skill as a Protestant propagandist won for him a symbolic place in the minds of his Catholic countrymen. In both North and South, he epitomised all that was reactionary in the Protestant planter tradition. Apart from answering for his personal sins, he became the target for all the grievances of the Catholic community, whether real or imaginary. Try as he might he could not divert attention to the other and more liberal aspects of his political life. In following the Orange and Protestant way he had been too successful; for Catholics throughout Ireland he *was* Ulster Unionism.

A typical and savage example of these pent-up feelings is revealed in the statement from Paddy Devlin MP a few days after internment was introduced in 1971. Even by Irish standards it was sturdy stuff, but it is a measure of the price which Faulkner has had to pay for years of partisan involvement in Northern Ireland's divided community. Devlin's outburst was volcanic: 'No one who has experience at first hand of this man would ever be fooled by his recent concern for his "Catholic fellow-countrymen". His own personal involvement in provocative demonstrations at Annalong and Dungiven show the real nature of the man. His cleverly contrived image of "Hardline" politician while climbing to power and his synthetic sweet reasonableness during the so-called reform era as a manipulator of propaganda is so clever in its use that he makes even Dr Goebbels seem second rate.' [13]

Such is the invective which Faulkner has attracted in his time.

But it is not the whole story. As the earlier tribute from G. B. Newe indicated, there was another side to Faulkner that was less well known by the Catholic community. But the Irish have long political memories and the sting in Devlin's comment, though based on the activities of previous decades, was a reminder to Faulkner that his earlier role had been noted by others than his co-religionists. Fortunately, the Irish also know how to forgive and start again. Not the least remarkable episode in the lives of these two turbulent Irish politicians, one a socialist Gael and the other a conservative Planter, was the way in which they overcame their differences to forge a close partnership in the first community government established for the Province in December 1973. Each had become a stout defender of the other.

For Faulkner the journey to the top had been a hazardous journey. Like all Unionist leaders he had collected his 'Orange card' on the way; by 1971 he had learned more fully than any of his predecessors that it could not be played with impunity in a divided community.

CHAPTER FOUR

1949——Election Special

It was not until 1941 that Brian Faulkner attended his first political meeting. For a young Tory it was an unusual choice— a Labour rally in South Belfast, with Harry Midgley, the noted Ulster socialist, as the main speaker.

Faulkner has never forgotten that first meeting and the excitement of the occasion. It was a fortunate introduction to local politics, giving him a glimpse of a new dimension in public affairs. It was also a non-sectarian dimension, which was to become increasingly rare in his life in the years ahead, but the message of one of Ireland's great Labour orators made a lasting impression; ever after, he had a deep respect for the Labour leader.

Harry Midgley was a household name in Ulster and at the height of his powers when Faulkner first heard him. Born in 1892, the Labour veteran was a 'University of Life' man, educated through hard experience in the shipyard and the first World War. He had known all the Labour 'greats'—men like William Walker, Keir Hardie, George Lansbury and Clement Attlee were among his closest political friends, and his service in workers' education, the Socialist Sunday School movement and Spanish Republican relief had won him a national reputation.

Faulkner also noted Midgley's love of knowledge. This love was deep and his desire to share it not less so. Indeed, a chance encounter with Midgley was like a stimulating university seminar; he handed out books and pamphlets with the childlike delight of the real lover of learning. Sometimes his books were more subtly given. On one occasion, when his shipyard foreman decided to suspend him for reading in the firm's time, he suggested that the boss should read the book before sending him home. On Monday morning the foreman returned the volume with a reprieve, remarking to the charge-hand: 'Keep your eye on that young fellow—he will go far.'

He did. The book was Jack London's *The Iron Heel*.

Such was the man who gave young Brian Faulkner his first glimpse of political life. Little wonder he was impressed; a man like this made Unionist politicians look decidedly parochial.

But Midgley's eloquence and fire were not enough to persuade Faulkner to change his allegiance—though, in future he was less ready to believe the 'red scare' tales told within his party about Labour leaders and was more ready than some of his colleagues to consider their ideas. In 1941 Midgley and Faulkner went their separate ways. Ironically, they did eventually become colleagues years later when Midgley 'crossed the floor' to become Minister of Labour and Minister of Education in Lord Brookeborough's post-war government.

Faulkner did not join his constituency Unionist Party until 1946 (the same year as he entered the Orange Order) when he became a member of the Mid-Down branch. This was an influential group counting as its members some of the most important county families. During this time he was also brought into contact with J. L. O. (later Sir John) Andrews, one of Ulster's most public spirited Unionists, with whom he established a close personal and political friendship which has held down the years and through many crises. By 1947 he had become secretary of the association and in the same year addressed his first meeting in the Strandtown Unionist Hall in East Belfast. It was the first of a long life of speaking engagements. He also became a rising star inside the Young Unionist Movement in which he competed for honours with ambitious young Tories as varied as Bill Craig, Brian McConnell and future Alliance Party convert, Stratton Mills.

Once started, Faulkner moved quickly. The immediate post-war world was a good time to enter Ulster politics. The war had ended and there was an air of excitement about as people streamed back from the forces with new ideas, determined to avoid the mistakes of their post-1918 parents. Throughout the British Isles there was a 'this is it' feeling among radicals in all groups.

Even conservative Ulster began to share in the excitement and to think of ways of continuing and deepening the Protestant and Catholic contacts made in battlefields all over the world and during air-raids on Ulster towns and factories. As the war drew to an end impressive political rallies were held in every town, and packed political meetings (even on a Sunday!) became a feature of Belfast's vast Hippodrome and other halls. From all over the Province the crowds came to hear the new reform gospel preached by local leaders like Bob Getgood, David Purdy and Jack Dorricott. They were regularly supported by national figures like Morrison, Bevin, Dalton, and Cripps.

Even the small local Communist Party managed to play to packed houses with Willie Gallagher, the Red Dean of Canterbury or Palme Dutt topping their bill. Meanwhile the Hammer and Sickle was flown in many parts of the capital city and thousands filed past the City Hall exhibition to see the famous Sword of Stalingrad.

In Ulster terms a revolution of rising social expectations had arrived.

For Unionist headquarters worse was to come. The Labour Party in Belfast won four seats in Parliament and in the staid middle-class Bloomfield constituency William McCullough, the Communist leader, polled a formidable 5802 votes against the well-known government candidate Lord Glentoran's 9995. The countryside was moving too as rural seats were gained by radical non-sectarian candidates.

Unionist leaders were shaken by this move to the left. A top-level conference was called to discuss the 'English disease' and it was agreed to mount a counter-attack in every town and village. With a Kitchener-like finger, Sir Basil Brooke (later Lord Brookeborough) beckoned his young guard and the powerful, traditional Ulster Unionist Party went into action on a Province-wide basis.

The response was formidable: the O'Neills, Clarkes, Grosvenors and Brookes were all there as was to be expected; so were the young businessmen and lawyers—Brian Faulkner, Morris May, Brian Maginess and William Craig; and further down the social line came the workers—even Ian Paisley emerged to do his stint as an election agent for the Party. The old guard had got its young recruits; a new generation of Unionism, dedicated to ensure the social *status quo* and to repel the 'strange' ideas coming from across the water, was being prepared. But it was a worrying time for Ulster Unionism. There were even suggestions by some that dominion status might be a way out of Attlee's socialist commonwealth; for, as the Ulster Prime Minister said in one memorable election speech, 'Only a bloody fool would vote Labour'!

The Unionist revival was thorough (Faulkner played a part in it and helped to produce a pamphlet of ideas on reorganisation) and within a few years the radical tide had been turned. The non-sectarian politics promised by the trade union and Labour upsurge of the 1940s were replaced by a return to the arid tribalism of the past; the literature of the Left Book Club brought back by the troops lost pride of place to Orange and Green pamphlets and the inter-denominational friendships forged in war began to fade under the pressures of sectarianism.

By 1949 it was all too clear that Ulster had witnessed a false dawn. The new era of welfare politics gave way to old-fashioned border debates as all Ireland, both North and South, was once again divided on issues which brought out the sectarian worst. It was a depressing reversal.

As Churchill said after a previous war: 'The whole map of Europe has been changed. The position of countries has been violently altered. The modes of thought of men, the whole outlook on affairs, the grouping of parties, all have encountered violent and tremendous changes in the deluge of the world, but as the deluge subsides and the waters fall short we see the dreary steeples of Fermanagh and Tyrone emerging once again. The integrity of their quarrel is one of the few institutions which has been unaltered in the cataclysm which has swept the world. That says a lot for the persistence with which Irish men on the one side or the other are able to pursue their controversies.' [14]

For Unionists and Nationalists the 1949 general election for Stormont was no disappointment. This was terrain they understood and they pursued their ancient controversies with enthusiasm. Orange and Green, the battle was engaged, while radical candidates lost their deposits in districts where, a few years earlier, they had been heroes.

Faulkner was fortunate in this election to find a nomination in an area he knew well—East Down. The selection meeting was held in the Assembly Rooms, Downpatrick, in January and several hundred delegates turned up. It was a choice seat, held by a well-known local military man, Colonel Gordon, who was retiring from politics. The competition was formidable—two ex-service candidates, Captain L. P. S. Orr (later Westminster MP for South Down) and Colonel Perceval Price. Their war record told in their favour, but they were meeting a professional in politics. Faulkner and his supporters had prepared the ground carefully and felt certain of the vote. Their optimism was justified and at the end of a two-hour meeting their nominee was selected by a large majority. Brian Faulkner had a seat for life.

That same night the new candidate for East Down had the good fortune to meet Jack McRobert, a local solicitor, who agreed to become his election agent. McRobert has done this voluntary service with outstanding success and skill for a quarter of a century. He is one of Faulkner's closest friends.

In the years immediately preceding 1949 Faulkner had been building up a reputation as a speaker at local Unionist rallies. The hard-hitting style he had developed was well suited to the kind of campaign offered by the 1949 election, and the image he had been creating for himself in Orange halls up and down the country fitted the occasion. Yet it was a pity that he had to start his career in such a negative and acrimonious atmosphere; for someone with leadership aspirations more mind-stretching issues were needed.

But by all accounts Faulkner enjoyed the campaign. He knew beforehand that his seat was safe, so he could relax and enjoy participation in some of the great 'gut' issues of Irish politics. The issues were emotive enough, for the decision of Eire to leave the Commonwealth and to declare for a republic involved problems of citizenship which concerned Northern Ireland. Sir Basil Brooke announced: Ulster must tell the world where she stood on the constitutional issue. So, once again the call went out, 'The border is in danger.'

In the 1949 election, as in so many others in Northern Ireland, normal politics were discounted and people were invited to take part in what was virtually a referendum on British citizenship, which, in turn became a counting of Protestant and Roman Catholic heads. Non-sectarian candidates were caught between the two main groups and the social and economic dialogue which had dominated the election of 1945 was forgotten in the communal confrontation organised by Ulster's Tories, Orange and Green alike.

Faulkner proved an enthusiastic campaigner and vied with his colleagues in producing rousing slogans, showing that he too could evoke memories of William of Orange, Carson and Craigavon.

Something of the flavour of the campaign is captured by the eve-of-poll advertisement in the *Belfast Telegraph* to which all Unionist candidates subscribed. In tone it was calculated to raise the political temperature and to produce a greatest-ever Protestant response; it was successful in both respects.

Election Manifesto

'Our country is in danger. We are fighting to defend our very existence and the heritage of our children.

The British Government will abide by the decision we make together. Therefore our loyalty must be overwhelmingly affirmed.

In the Dail the other day a gentleman said the gun would be used. We are not going to be scared.

We are perfectly capable of looking after ourselves.

I want to assure you that the Government will see to it that law and order will be maintained.

We are a friendly people, but we are not going to be threatened.

We are not going into a Gaelic state.

We are not going to ask our children to learn a Gaelic language.

We are not going to have lower social services.

We shall defend Ulster with the last bit of life left in us.

So I call on you to give an answer to our opposition at the poll that will resound throughout the world.

That answer will be "No Surrender".'

Even allowing for the tensions of 1949 this was colourful language, but there is no evidence that any of the bright young men recruited by Unionist headquarters wished to modify it.

Later at a pre-election rally in the Ulster Hall Sir Basil Brooke made his own stirring appeal: 'I ask you to cross the Boyne, if you like, with me as your leader and to fight for the same cause as King William fought in the days gone by. My friends, my soldiers march with me. Your battle cry is "No Surrender". We are King's men.'

Even Somerville and Ross would have been hard put to equal such as this.

In the midst of such heady stuff Faulkner showed that he appreciated a fuller range of argument. He did not hesitate to deal with wider issues stretching well beyond the County Down. He also saw that he was well reported and then, as in the years to come, he prepared his press material with great care. It is also significant that even at this stage in his career several of the big county names joined his campaign.

One notable visitor was Terence O'Neill, who came to the local Orange hall to support the new recruit. He, too, was caught up in the excitement of the time and in a resounding final flourish called upon the local voters: 'Count your blessings. Count your votes and give East Down the largest majority ever.' Years later he may have regarded the victory as a mixed blessing!

During his first campaign Faulkner concentrated on the theme of British citizenship. He saw this as the central issue and agreed that Ulster must proclaim to the world its resolve 'not to enter into union with the Irish Republic'. As he put it: 'Our duty is to say to the Universe that we will have no truck with the Republic and on this question we are the arbiters irrespective of the views of any other state.' This last reference was taken as a warning to the Attlee administration that there should be no tampering with fundamental citizenship rights.

It was the first of many which he was to send to British governments, Labour and Conservative alike.

It was also a hands off warning to the Dublin government, and it reveals an aspect of Faulkner's thinking which has remained constant. He has been ready at all times to co-operate with the South, but only on terms which do not involve a surrender of Northern sovereignty on constitutional matters. Down the years he has worked hard to persuade both Dublin and London to take his advice on this matter. In 1949 United Kingdom citizenship was a particularly sensitive subject, for the Dublin government, through Mr Sean McBride, Minister for External Affairs, had involved itself in the Northern election and had helped to create an all-party anti-partition fund. The extraordinary step was taken to organise a national collection throughout all parishes on a Sunday before the poll—hence the name, 'Chapel Door Collection Election'.

McBride's intervention made a Unionist victory certain and provided many quotations which Faulkner and his colleagues used happily for many years to come. A typical remark on which Unionists were able to fasten was McBride's seal of approval on the all-party fund: 'It is the first real sign of unity since 1921. I know that from glen to glen, parish to parish, from town to town the people of Ireland will look upon this development with hope and a throb in their hearts and will pray for its success.'

As an exercise in political ineptitude the Southern intervention in the 1949 Ulster election could not have been equalled. Certainly there was a response from every glen and parish in the North, but it was a Unionist response, giving the Party its biggest-ever victory since the foundation of the state.

In the landslide return for Unionists Faulkner had a safe majority:

1949 Election, East Down

A. B. D. Faulkner (Unionist)	8132
K. McGrady (Nationalist)	5480
Majority	2652

Twenty years later, in 1969, things had changed little, though then there was also a pro-O'Neill Unionist:

A. B. D. Faulkner	8136
K. McGrady	6427
Lt. Col. Rowan Hamilton	1248
Faulkner majority	1709

Four years later in the June 1973 Assembly Election (South Down), fought under proportional representation, Faulkner obtained a massive first preference vote of 16,287, exceeded in the whole Province only by James Kilfedder (20,484) in much larger North Down, and well ahead of his most formidable rivals Ian Paisley (14,533) and William Craig (8538).

But in 1949 the more complicated permutations of PR and community government were far from the mind of the new member for East Down. The old order seemed very permanent as he told his constituents: 'East Down will tell Mr Costello and the rest of them that they resent meddlesome interference from a foreign power. They will give them the answer of the Thirteen Apprentice Boys of Derry—"No Surrender".'

During the campaign he had learned the political vocabulary thoroughly and would continue to use it when he deemed it necessary. But he also took care to remind his electors that there was another side to the bargain which he had struck with them. He insisted on his right to talk about more than the Constitution. Politics was certainly about 'the spiritual freedom of every man and woman' but it was also important to be concerned about 'the prices our farmers receive for their produce, the wages our men are paid, the pensions and benefits for the old, the infirm and the widows'. He was pledged to uphold the Constitution, 'but on domestic matters I reserve the right to criticise where I see just cause'.

As they say in Ulster, the half-crown as well as the Crown had to be watched. Faulkner has never forgotten this fact of life and never fails to stress it.

But though he won his 1949 contest Faulkner could have taken little satisfaction from it. Like most Unionists and

Nationalists of his day, the chief hurdle was to win the nomination. Then, according to the 'tribal' count, the result was predictable. In fact, in Northern Ireland few open contests were possible until PR. Faulkner's real political struggles were to be inside the Unionist Party; Nationalists might oppose him at the polls but they could not hope to defeat him.

The 1949 general election gave the first clear indication of Faulkner's political style. It was a style that has changed little down the years. Certainly he was prepared, like the rest of his colleagues, 'to beat the drum', but beyond the histrionics there was a cautious conservative who also saw the necessity to protect the social and economic fabric of the society in which the drum-beating took place. Later, he was to learn that too much drum-beating was itself a threat to the social framework.

The years in industry had not been in vain; the practical philosophies of his father and grandmother had left their mark; perhaps, even, some of Harry Midgley's social message had made an impression.

CHAPTER FIVE

The Power and the Glory

The Stormont that Brian Faulkner entered in 1949 was very different from the Assembly he was to lead in 1974. Ulster's 'best club' was dominated by the county families, many with Anglo-Irish traditions and with a strong sprinkling of Eton and the Guards. The 'Big House' still ruled and even the most prosperous of the Protestant middle-class were regarded in the 1940s as merely *nouveau riche*. Social rebels were appearing on the Unionist side to challenge the old structure, but, as many found to their cost, Ulster, too, had a magic circle which was not easily broken.

Most Ulster Unionists (especially those with Presbyterian backgrounds) resented this assumption of power by the landed gentry and sought to change it. But their insistence on change was limited by the demand to maintain Party unity in the face of a divide more obvious than class and one which cut horizontally across the Province—the sectarian separation of the people into Protestant and Catholic religious camps. Those who sought to change the traditional power structure were warned that internal divisions among Protestants would increase the danger of a Nationalist take-over. Catholic radicalism was held in check by tribal arguments based on the same assumptions of sectarianism.

The Stormont Parliament was, in fact, based on confrontation politics—on the sectarian assumption that it was natural for Ulster people to divide on religious grounds. Bridge-building groups were regarded as being unimportant. What emerged after 1920, and was often encouraged to emerge, was a people divided against itself—born apart, living apart, worshipping apart and whose children played apart and learnt apart. What was needed during the formative years of the Northern Irish

45

State was a politics of partnership, with political principles and structures dedicated to the task of creating a united Province where there could be Government partnership between the Protestant and Catholic communities. This opportunity was not taken by the founding fathers of the state. So Ulster was set on a collision course from its inception. Material progress was made but the fatal community flaw was never tackled.

When Brian Faulkner entered the House of Commons in February 1949 he gave no indication that he was aware of these problems and, like most politicians of his day, whether Unionist or Nationalist, he seemed resigned to accept the framework inside which he was born: in the words of an Ulsterism, he had no intention of 'jumping out of the bowl he was baked in'.

During the first seven years in Stormont he was content to build up a reputation as a House of Commons man and a good constituency member with, as we have seen, an active role in the Orange Order. His early speeches were wide ranging with particular emphasis on trade and industry. Little attention was paid to political theories and, in general, his approach reflected the sturdy independence of the Ulster family-farm man, suspicious of state and trade union intervention, while on regional problems he took a traditional Protestant ascendancy position.

In style of speaking Faulkner adopted a matter of fact approach, concentrating on content rather than presentation and employing much carefully arranged detailed material to support his case. When speaking he sticks close to his theme and is not easily deflected by interruption. Sometimes the concentration can be remarkable. During his Sunningdale report speech of December 1973[17], for instance, he was interrupted 120 times in twenty-four minutes (surely a parliamentary record!) yet as one skips the interruptions the Hansard Report reads smoothly and the closely knit argument continues uninterrupted. Perhaps unfortunately for Faulkner, in a country which appreciates both, he is not given to wit or emotion in speech—here, apt comparisons have been made with the equally neat and formal style of Liam Cosgrave.

In recent years Faulkner has mellowed a great deal though by popular Irish standards he remains something of an aesthetic. His wife and family and the daily present of the intellectual and more worldly young aides with whom he has surrounded himself have done much to redress the public image in his favour.

Much of this businesslike style was in evidence in Faulkner's early speeches to the Ulster Commons. His maiden speech[18] was delivered on 15 March 1949 and took place on the parochial, but, for Faulkner, apt, subject of the future of railways in his beloved County Down. He took the opportunity to say something about the special needs of his constituency and also to relate the future of transport to the future of the whole Province. He used plenty of factual material (a favourite practice) and even managed to liken the Transport Authority to the College of Cardinals and its head to the Pope. Happily it was a light-hearted reference and all sides received him well. He was praised warmly for his effort by another new and older member, Morris May, who was to have considerable influence on him in later years. Thereafter, he was a frequent speaker in the Ulster Commons.

During his days as a backbencher Faulkner established himself as a hard-hitting and competent debater. Whether as private member or as Chief Whip (which he became in 1956) he was never faulted on his attention to detail and his ability to work hard.

Fortunately for Faulkner he was noticed early on in his career by Lord Brookeborough, the Ulster Premier. One of the shrewdest politicians Ulster has known, Lord Brookeborough kept his party together during some of the most critical days in its history and helped to produce a new team of post-war Unionist leaders. Unfortunately he took an *après moi le déluge* view of life and failed to read the new times aright. With his great authority he could have done much to bridge the North/South and the Protestant/Catholic gaps; what a different history Ulster and all of Ireland might have had if de Valera and Brookeborough in the 1950s rather than O'Neill and Lemass in the 1960s had got together.

But Brookeborough had undoubtedly an ability to spot talent, and very soon in his career Faulkner was being awarded prestige-speaking parts in the House. By the general election of 1953 he began to emerge as a Unionist leader and his elevation to the position of Chief Whip in 1956 came as no surprise. Three years later his appointment as Minister of Home Affairs was equally expected.

When Faulkner took over Home Affairs in 1959, he decided to devote himself entirely to politics. He resigned from the family business and thereafter became a full-time politician. This was a key move, and in his day somewhat unusual among Unionists in government, who preferred to mix business with the political life. It marked him out (like O'Neill) as a dedicated professional and gave him an edge on most of his colleagues who combined their departments with other occupations.

Home Affairs was a considerable challenge as a first ministry. It was generally regarded as Stormont's most difficult post and very much an emotional minefield. Few career politicians relished the job and the appointment generally went to a lawyer who aspired to higher legal office. With only six months of legal training behind him, Faulkner had no such ambitions; typically he 'liked the challenge of the job'. He was given a free hand to meet the challenge by the Prime Minister, who told him on appointment: 'It is your Department and your responsibility. So long as you keep within Party policy you will have my support at all times.' This was typical of Brookeborough's leadership style. Faulkner appreciated the trust implied; he became one of Brookeborough's firmest supporters.

When Faulkner took office he was faced immediately with two of Ulster's most controversial fields of policy—security and franchise reform. As a result, during his four years of service he found life very much a political treadmill. It was also an experience which isolated him increasingly from the community, for he was forced to engage in discussions which involved him with communally emotive subjects. Defending as he did the traditional Unionist view, he very soon developed a 'hard-line' image among the community in general and with

Catholics in particular. He did not complain; it was an occupational hazard that went with the job.

Home Affairs did, of course, offer constructive opportunities, but unfortunately for Faulkner he took over at a time when security problems were to the fore. When he came to office the IRA campaign of the 1950s was still in operation and law and order matters dominated the department. He took readily to the responsibility and soon proved to be an inflexible opponent of the terrorist. Then, as ever after, he insisted that a successful security policy was essential for success in government.

In a speech to the Commons a few months after his appointment, Faulkner outlined his views on the security situation. He fully accepted the general security policy of the Unionist Party and felt that there was no alternative to the policies which had been pursued down the years. He believed in firmness and was convinced that 'an integral part of those security precautions has been the internment of persons who we had reason to believe were prepared to use force for illegal means'. He was, at the same time, happy to announce that since he had come to office and considered it in the interest of the country to do so, he had ordered the release of internees. As he put it: 'This is a happy situation and I hope it will not be necessary to use our power of internment in future.' He also warned that anyone who considered becoming involved in subversive activity should think 'well and long before setting out upon such a course'. His warning was clear: 'I will not hesitate to use the power of internment in respect of anyone who does become active in the work of the IRA or other kindred organisations. I am satisfied that internment coupled with the setting up of comprehensive security precautions has been effective in frustrating the aims of the enemies of our state.'

The 1950s IRA campaign and his involvement in its termination had a lasting influence on Faulkner's approach to security matters. It was, in fact, for him a very short war, but it came to an end during his Ministry and he seemed to find it a satisfying experience. Ever after, he (and a wide public, too) was sure that he had got the measure of his foe and knew how to deal with them. He felt confident, too, in the tactics employed and believed that internment and the other comprehensive security precautions employed had been the key to success. He gave much less weight to the important fact that the campaign had been confined, in the main, to the country areas of the Province and had received little local support. However, he was proud of his success and became something of a folk hero among his party and Orange Order colleagues because of it. He was also sure that he could repeat the process if called upon to do so. Years later, as Prime Minister of Northern Ireland, he was to lean heavily on this experience and belief to deal with another terrorist campaign, but this time in the very different circumstances of the 1970s.

He was also anxious as Minister of Home Affairs to involve the South of Ireland in joint responsibility for what was happening security-wise in the North and was deeply offended when there was evidence that the Southern government was either ignoring illegal organisations or correcting them with rods of straw. So: 'It is a disgraceful state of affairs in a country that assumes itself to be largely Christian, that such people can be roaming about. In addition, sentences with a maximum of six months that have been given by the courts in Eire are in my view no deterrent to men taking part in these illegal activities.' [20] Fourteen years later, when defending the Sunningdale agreement as Chief Executive in the Northern Ireland Assembly, he was still emphatic that the South had a key role to play in the campaign against the terrorist. In a speech to the Assemblymen (19 March 1974) he complained that Northerners had been deeply affected by 'the ambivalence of many Southern attitudes towards the campaign of violence'. What he wanted to see for the defeat of terrorism was 'wholehearted action in and by the Irish Republic'. In addition, the average Ulsterman wanted 'real action, not a lot of talk about fugitive offenders' where terrorists hiding out in the South were concerned. The average Ulsterman wanted to see 'open, well-organised, properly co-ordinated joint action along the Border'. Time had not altered his problem or the remedy.

At all times, both before and since his elevation to top office, Faulkner has been careful to insist that the recognised security forces, and they alone, should have the responsibility for the enforcement of law and order. He has been suspicious of vigilante groups and for him the formidable security force controlled by his ministry was enough. He was always quick to parry criticism of the forces under his control and to call on the public to support them: 'May I appeal from the depth of my heart to the loyalists of Northern Ireland to show by their continued, let alone dignified, restraint their absolute faith in the RUC, the USC and the security forces generally and to treat these young men of the IRA with the contempt of which they are only worthy.' [21] The RUC, in particular, has always been held high in his regard and he was a popular minister with the force.

In dealing with the problem of security Faulkner could argue that he was dealing with a situation which was peculiar to his part of the United Kingdom and to which there was an established response laid down by his predecessors in office. When faced with criticisms of his policy (especially when reservations came from Britain) he argued that he was the victim of local circumstances which required extraordinary measures. In general, successive British governments were prepared to let this argument go unchallenged. But there were many other aspects of Home Affairs to which such an argument could not conceivably apply. Here, again, the Minister had an opportunity to introduce reforms and attempt to give a lead to the more backward members of his party. The chance was not taken.

On the question of the local government franchise, for example, Faulkner took the old-fashioned conservative attitude that only the rate-payer should have a say at City Hall. Regardless of progressive post-war changes in the British voting system, he was prepared to argue that Ulster should not agree to such reforms. Even before he became a minister his views were inflexible: 'It is the people with a stake in the country who should have a vote at local government elections. Would anyone honestly suggest that if non-property owners were given the vote they would be as careful about the expenditure of rate-payers money and that they would see that people were elected who would be as careful about ratepayers money as the ratepayers themselves?' [22] Or more bluntly: 'Successive ministers have frequently enumerated the principle that it is fair that those who pay the piper should call the tune. I hold that view.'

This belief in the link between ownership of property and its efficient use was emphatic: 'I suggest that our objective must be to get on to local councils people who are representative of the widest possible range of persons directly interested and with some recognizable stake in the welfare of the country. One cannot get such an electorate merely by swelling the numbers of the electorate by simply giving the vote to a greater number of people.' [23] When the view was pressed on him that increased representation elsewhere had not led to a reduction in standard of service he fell back on the argument of leaving well alone: 'The present system has worked admirably for all the citizens of Northern Ireland.' Here he blandly ignored the fact that the political organisations of the entire non-Unionist community were pressing for franchise reform.

On other occasions Faulkner even argued against a change on the grounds that opposition members were being party political in their demands. He was insistent that the system had operated 'equitably and satisfactorily and efficiently'. In these circumstances why change it? Was it because it would be to the advantage of the opposition? At no point did it seem to occur to the Minister that even if the system were efficient a most important democratic principle was at stake. In any case, it did not need a Lord Cameron, even in the 1960s, to recognise the deep-seated and dangerous defects of local government in Northern Ireland. Plenty of local voices, especially from the non-sectarian trade union and Labour movement, were urging the Minister and his party to adopt reforms which were generally accepted throughout the rest of the United Kingdom. By not seeking to change the policy of the Unionist Party in this area Faulkner missed an opportunity for significant leadership. Ironically, years later, he was to resign from O'Neill's cabinet on this same issue, and eventually as Minister of Development he carried through a considerable reform of local government against the opposition of many of his own supporters. By then he was acting wisely, but was doing it after a period of acute communal tension and pressure from Westminster. In consequence, he got little credit for the reforms promoted.

While Faulkner chided the opposition in the 1960s for their desire to increase their electoral influence by seeking to extend the franchise, he did not hesitate to defend the privileged position of his own party in Queen's University where, for many years, it benefited from a university franchise which granted Queen's four seats in the Ulster House of Commons. He believed that it was 'worthwhile that these young people should be given this slight additional voice in the representation of this House'.[25] But it was no small voice: it was four seats out of fifty-two, and since the Unionist Party always won at least two of these seats there was a considerable political advantage to be gained from university representation. Neither the Minister nor his party considered it incongruous that 80,000 people in Belfast should be denied a local government vote while 12,091 graduates at the university could claim a sizeable parliamentary representation.

All in all, the Minister's record on franchise was inglorious, and years later the issue gave an effective cutting-edge to the civil rights campaign.

Faulkner's views were also put to the test on another important public issue during his period as Minister of Home Affairs: capital punishment. Throughout his career law and order had been a central concern. He was ever anxious to see that nothing was done to weaken the coercive powers of the state in the battle against crime; capital punishment, he believed, was utterly essential. His views on the subject were the stock-in-trade of the traditional opponent of abolition and they have changed little during his lifetime. In an important debate in the Ulster Commons (13 February 1962) he outlined his views, personal as well as departmentally. He saw capital punishment as 'a great deterrent' and felt it a duty to retain the death penalty for murder 'simply and solely from a sense of duty to the public'. He dismissed the views of those who argued to the contrary and believed that it was his duty to have regard to the state of public opinion. He was also profoundly suspicious of those who, according to him, made up their minds on what he called 'emotional rather than logical considerations'. Here there was not the slightest recognition that honest emotion and sound logic might go together.

Even his regard for church leaders did not prevent him from putting them in their place, which, he seemed to think, was in the pulpit and not in the market place: 'Some church leaders have spoken out against capital punishment. Their views command and deserve the greatest respect from all of us. Their vocation leads them to look at this problem from an altogether different view to the layman and different also from those who are responsible for the maintenance of law and order. The layman is much more likely to be informed by a sense of natural justice clearly geared to human values and to be strongly influenced by the need to protect the innocent from the vicious.' It says much for the Christian charity of Ulster's clergy that the Minister was able to get away with this sort of reasoning. Quite apart from the fact that many of the most important opponents of the hanging law were, in fact, laymen, the passage showed an extraordinary example of a double-standard approach.

In his final ministerial contribution to the subject, given a few months before he left Home Affairs, Faulkner did not modify his views. Capital punishment remained 'the great deterrent' and he claimed that those 'brought into close contact with criminal elements in the population believe that the fear of being hanged is a sizeable deterrent to violence'. He asked members before they voted to look at the matter from 'the objective view of what is best for society as a whole'. He did, however, on this occasion, leave the subject to a free vote of the House. But he had no need to worry; his colleagues were behind him, only two breaking rank.

During his term of office Faulkner's opinions on capital punishment were put firmly to the test. No less than four times in one year he had to advise the Governor of Northern Ireland on the prerogative power of mercy. Only two of the persons involved were reprieved. It cannot be said that he did not accept the awesome responsibility that went with his attitude.

The subjects of security, voting rights and capital punishment were the main areas of controversy for Faulkner during his period in Home Affairs and earned him no reputation as an innovator. But, less noticed, there were also considerable advances in penal reform. He was able to claim credit for new approaches to the treatment of young offenders and, in particular, his open borstal system attracted favourable comment. A new system of parole for long-term prisoners was also introduced with considerable success.

Transfer from the Ministry of Home Affairs came in 1963. It had been a hard spell and, unlike former ministers who were able to escape to the Bench, Faulkner had to continue a political career. When he left, his civil servants felt he had been a fair and efficient minister, who could hold his own at any Cabinet meeting. In the words of one of his top advisers: 'A hard man to get to know, but the best I have ever worked for. A fantastic memory, with more energy than ten of us and absolutely unafraid to take a hard decision and stick by it. He fought like a tiger for his Department and everyone in it.'

Public-wise he had emerged as a tough minister. Among Unionists he was regarded as one who would not let the side down; opponents saw him as a force to be reckoned with, 'the toughest Unionist of them all'. However, his first ministerial post had given him the status he needed in the Unionist Party. From now on he was on the leadership ladder.

Then in 1963 he was called upon to do a job he really cared and knew about—Commerce. Home Affairs had given him the power; now he felt he could achieve the glory.

Faulkner was well suited to the Commerce post. His years in the textile trade and his knowledge of Ulster's biggest industry, agriculture, were valuable; furthermore, he and his family were regarded by the business community as people who understood their problems and who had shared a considerable stake in the commercial life of the Province. Faulkner also welcomed the promotion as a happy release from the emotional treadmill offered in Home Affairs. Now he could relax again

and display the side of him which he regarded as paramount—
the man of industrial affairs. And he was shrewd enough to
realise that a reputation as a job-getter would give him strong
support among every sector of the Ulster population. He was
also fortunate to be moving into Commerce at a take-off point
in the Province—the beginning of a decade of new social and
economic expansion for which plans were already being
assembled. Westminster, too, was encouraging a policy of
regional development. It was a good time to be Minister of
Commerce.

The new minister went about his work methodically. Again,
he had been given a free hand by the Prime Minister, a fact
which he appreciated. He immediately strengthened the
research facilities of his ministry and top-level economists were
commissioned to produce a series of reports on the economy.
Civil servants who believed in this approach were recruited and
given rapid promotion. Under the new scheme of things management and unions were brought together in a regional
economic council, and a joint operation was mounted to
analyse the findings of the economists and to establish long-term
objectives for the economic development of the Province.
Before long, Commerce came to be regarded as the most
dynamic of Ulster's ministries and even the English regions
began to ask that similar industrial initiatives be introduced on
the Ulster pattern.

Faulkner saw clearly that the industrial base of the Province
would have to be widened and he very quickly convinced his
fellow industrialists that pride in the past must not come before
profits for the future. He recognised that new-type industries
were needed and that new markets for the resultant products
would have to be found. He promised every possible aid to
industry and was soon able to boast that Northern Ireland
was 'a step ahead' of every other part of the United Kingdom
in this respect. He also attempted to push new industrial developments away from Belfast and became a pioneer of the 'new
growth point' campaign in the Province. The question of new
industries was a politically sensitive one, for Catholics argued
that the wealth of the Province was concentrated in the eastern

and more Protestant areas. Faulkner denied that he encouraged this concentration and stressed that he could not direct incoming industry into specified areas, but he did promise that every assistance would be given to industrialists who would go to the underdeveloped areas of Northern Ireland.

He cites as two important examples of his West of the Bann interest the offer of £1 million extra in grants to the Michelin Tyre Company if they would take a site in the Londonderry area and the equally 'tremendous pressure' exerted on the Carreras Tobacco Company to locate their factory outside the Belfast area.

It was true, of course, that incoming industry could not be forced into a particular site, but the chronic unemployment in the western areas of the Province were still in stark contrast to the boom conditions elsewhere. Many of the most depressed areas were anti-Unionist politically and obviously this added to the political urgency of encouraging enterprises suitable for such problem zones. Unfortunately the Ministry of Commerce was reluctant to move in with government-sponsored enterprise and Faulkner share this reluctance. He was willing to pay considerable sums in subsidies or in unemployment benefit, but he drew the line where direct intervention was concerned. In general, his approach was that of helping private industry to do its task efficiently and to provide the conditions in which it could flourish. As he put it: 'Hundreds of thousands of electors in Great Britain seem to support the theory that the maximum of assistance should be given to private enterprise and seemed to be very concerned about any threat of widespread nationalisation.' He was speaking in the aftermath of substantial Tory majorities in Britain.

Even where pilot schemes were concerned he had his doubts. He was willing to tolerate pilot schemes as a way of assisting the development of the natural resources of the country (water, afforestation, mineral research) but where manufacturing was concerned he drew a clear line—private enterprise remained the supreme consideration.

He also claimed that such opposition had nothing to do with political doctrine and refuted all charges of mixing politics with business. On one occasion he told Stormont (7.4.65) that his guide-line on projects was 'first, is it calculated to be of benefit to the people of Northern Ireland; and, secondly, and perhaps of equal importance, will it work?' Unfortunately for those who advocated state schemes he never regarded their suggestions as meeting his guide-line standard! As he put it, frankly and firmly: 'I am against state concern in manufacturing because I do not believe it will work.' Later on in his career, however, he did encourage a good deal of state involvement with the industry of the Province, and it was under his premiership that the Government of Northern Ireland became a major shareholder in the local shipyard. And when he became Chief Executive in 1974, one of his first promises as leader of the new administration was to ensure that the Province would be provided with 'new machinery developed to facilitate Government involvement in promising industrial enterprises and ventures, which offer the prospect of new and expanding employment opportunities'.

But even Faulkner's most constant critics have had to acknowledge his record of achievement as Minister of Commerce. He was true to his conservative principles, but at the same time he managed to establish a new and firm industrial base for the Province which has stood up well to the pressures occasioned by political strife. He was also able to maintain good relationships with London ministers, whether Conservative or Labour. With the Labour government which held office during his years as a minister he was on good terms, and speaks warmly of the assistance which he received from George Brown, Roy Jenkins, Douglas Jay and James Callaghan. With Harold Wilson there was less contact, but after the various confrontations with Mr Heath in 1972 and 1973 he had no difficulty in adjusting to the change of government in 1974. Indeed, when Harold Wilson took up residence again in Downing Street, one of his first callers was Brian Faulkner and the Chief Executive was quick to indicate that he would be happy to work with the new administration.

At times, particularly during the early years of his ministry he was less able to get on with the local representatives of the labour movement and until the recognition of the Irish Congress of Trade Unions during O'Neill's premiership he was regarded as unhelpful when government/union relations arose. In 1963 he opposed a motion which came before the Commons to set up an 'all-party committee to examine and make proposals to resolve the deadlock in the relations between the Northern Ireland Government and workers' organisations'. This opposition was deeply resented by the unions and made them cautious of his other overtures. No doubt, as he argues, Faulkner was following party policy, but he missed an opportunity to give a lead on this issue and to make a firm relationship with trade union leaders. Later on, when he got to know the trade union leaders personally, mutual respect developed and his drive for new jobs received strong support from the local TUC.

One of the great success stories of his years in Commerce was his plan to bring new-type industries to the Province. This was part of his plan to diversify industrially and to enable the Province to take advantage of new growth industries. An example of his foresight in this field followed a visit to the United States in 1964 where he met Henry Ford and discussed the potential of the car components industry. Ford pointed out that any area with a properly developed components industry was well placed to become a centre for a complete car assembly industry. Faulkner took the hint and today Good Year, Autolite, Michelin and Rolls-Royce are well established in the Province. He hopes eventually to see a complete car being produced in Northern Ireland—'an Ulster car on every road'.

The visit to Detroit to see Ford was typical of Faulkner's sales visits for his ministry. He became Ulster's most travelled minister and combed the world for new enterprises. In the process he built up a formidable sales team abroad and with their assistance produced inducements for foreign firms which were tailormade to suit local needs. Foreign industrialists have appreciated this very personal service in the fields of special subsidies and training and a relationship has been built up which has done much to offset the difficulties inherent in the geographical position of the area.

Two years after his transfer to Commerce Faulkner was able

to announce an economic plan offering a new frontier of economic progress for the Province. In a fifty-minute speech to the Commons he promised 65,000 new jobs in five years and full-scale modernisation for the shipyard along with a new dry dock for Belfast. Advance factories were being prepared for the west and other peripheral areas and he looked forward to making Londonderry a modern industrial region. Exploitation of natural resources was not forgotten and he promised a greatly expanded exploration programme. Even for the trade unions there were firm assurances. The difficulties with the Dublin-based Irish Congress of Trade Unions were forgotten: 'I regard relations with the ICTU as harmonious and regard them as extremely valuable. I like to think that I have its confidence. Certainly I hope it feels it shares mine.'

This was a new Faulkner, transformed by the challenge of a ministry he felt to be his own. And the changed look evoked a changed response in the House. All sides rose to praise him. From the Nationalist spokesman came the comment: 'One would be churlish not to give credit to the Minister for his dynamic leadership and consistent hard work.' The Labour leader praised the optimistic tone of the speech and promised the support of his movement.

But most welcome of all was the warm praise of Mr Gerry Fitt: 'I believe it is generally conceded that the Minister since becoming Minister of Commerce has been a great asset. He has done everything possible to attract more industries and I feel that every section of the community must commend him for the very energetic way in which he carries out the duties of his office.' Fitt also praised him for his new approach to the trade unions: 'I should also like to congratulate the Minister on the very harmonious relations which exist between his Department and the ICTU. I know that it took him a long time to bring about the present policy set-up between the Ministry and the unions. The Minister would be the first to concede that anticipated troubles proved to be non-existent and long may this trend continue.' Coming from a life-long political opponent this was fulsome praise indeed; in the light of developments between the two men years later it was a significant comment.

But perhaps the most telling comment came from a Labour backbencher who observed that Faulkner's was the kind of speech that might have come from opposition benches some five or six years earlier and was evidence of the way in which the minister had managed to move the industrial policy of the Unionist Party in the meantime. The same member also observed that the statement was 'not so much a speech as a bid for leadership—a clever speech and perhaps another nail in the coffin of some of his rivals'.[29]

By 1965, in the eyes of many both inside and outside Stormont, Faulkner's role as a Commerce Minister had confirmed them in their judgement that he was the man to lead the Province into the next phase of its history. Unfortunately for him his success had come too late to prevent the elevation of O'Neill on the resignation of Brookeborough. He was now deputy to Terence O'Neill, but it was a partnership more of shared convenience than of mutual respect. Properly harnessed, they could have made a formidable team; but as they were, they constituted an irritant to each other and a dangerous division at the centre of power at a crucial point in Ulster's history.

In the remaining years of his Commerce Ministry under O'Neill Faulkner continued to fill his office with distinction, with assured support from the leaders of the industrial community. Even during the worst of the crisis he managed to insulate his department from the political strife and the economy continued to improve. In fact, Ulster during the worst political crisis in its history has been a paradox: industrial expansion and prosperity in the midst of social and political chaos.

By 1969 O'Neill and Faulkner had become increasingly disenchanted with each other and even the attractions of the Ministry of Commerce could not persuade the latter to remain in office. He resigned on 24 January 1969 and the exchange of letters between him and the Prime Minister revealed a depth of mutual misunderstanding which was a measure of the incompatibility of these two men, each equally anxious to serve their country.

Yet, in many ways the O'Neill/Faulkner clash was to be

expected. Each represented a powerful segment of Ulster life and each followed differing lifestyles, political and otherwise, which reflected those backgrounds. They did not attempt a cross-fertilisation; they never seemed to understand or respect each other. Perhaps from the very beginning these two ambitious politicians were on a collision course; certainly by 1969 it was clear that there would be no accommodation by one for the other.

CHAPTER SIX

O'Neill and Faulkner—the Cementing of a Rivalry

On 2 March 1962 the delicate balance within the Ulster Unionist Party was altered dramatically by the death of its most outstanding man of action and intellect, William Morrison May, Minister of Education. His death was sudden and, coming as it did at the early age of fifty-three, the Province was deprived of a Unionist leader who, more than any other, had the blend of qualities needed for the political era in which he lived.

Morris May had a wider appeal than any of his rivals. He had been born into the working-class and after winning for himself a first-class education he achieved a brilliant career as an accountant and company director. By his 'forties he had amassed a large fortune and was regarded as one of Ireland's most influential financiers, with good contacts in the City of London. Furthermore, he had the right 'image' among Unionists. His good service record, quiet, but loyal membership of the Orange Order, combined with personal charm and political drive gave him a freedom and authority denied to any of his rivals. In any community such a man would have been missed, but in a small society like Ulster the loss was a public disaster.

As the *Belfast Telegraph* put it on the night of his death: 'A Unionist couched in moderate terms and with a constant eye to the needs of the future. The feeling today that he will be extremely hard to replace is a just measure of the man.'

More important, Morris May was confident of his ability to succeed Brookeborough; and, vital factors, he had the measure of Terence O'Neill and the respect of Brian Faulkner. With him as leader, all three could have formed a successful working relationship. Nor could May have been passed over readily. He had already got from Brookeborough a guarantee that the succession would be decided at a full meeting of the Parliamentary Unionist Party.[30] This promise was all that May required; the support of moderate Unionists, along with Faulkner's support, would have given him powerful backing. With such a candidate available Terence O'Neill could never rank higher than an heir presumptive. Certainly, May never feared O'Neill as a rival, and his combination of wealth, talent and influence could not have been equalled by any other candidate from the 'Big House'.

But once the massive presence of the Minister of Education was removed all this changed. O'Neill assumed a new significance and he, too, began to loom larger than any of his rivals. Politics' oldest adage, 'where there is death there is hope', had intervened.

For Faulkner the death of his friend was felt politically as well as personally. He and May had come into politics in the same general election, had made their maiden speeches on the same day and had moved up the political ladder together as close colleagues. The younger politician had learned much from the older and more urbane man of the world. Faulkner had always enjoyed working with May and, his junior by a generation, had no intention of competing for the premiership against him. He had always expected to work alongside his friend; the sudden tragedy caught him unprepared.

O'Neill on the other hand had long been hoping for the premiership. When Brookeborough resigned a year after May's death, O'Neill was well placed to take over. The transfer of power was sudden and decisive. In March 1963 Brookeborough resigned, and before the Province had recovered from the sudden shock it was announced that the Governor of Northern Ireland had asked Terence O'Neill to form a new administration. The Unionist Party was particularly surprised to have been by-passed, but there was little that could be done without a major revolt. It was an Ulster version of the Douglas-Home/Butler incident; proof that Northern Ireland had its own 'magic circle'. The 'Big House' had had its way once again.

But O'Neill's method of coming to power deeply offended his parliamentary colleagues who had expected a democratic vote for the selection. Faulkner was also opposed to the method of selection and believed that it cut across the understanding which May and other Unionist leaders had established with Lord Brookeborough. Consequently, many Unionists felt that O'Neill had been imposed on the party. This greatly weakened their allegiance. Brookeborough subsequently indicated that he had mentioned three names (O'Neill, Faulkner, Andrews) to the Governor and asked him to make his choice. But few doubted at the time that the claim of O'Neill had been given the decisive push at the right moment. Faulkner, however, retained his warm affection for Brookeborough and though he disagreed with his judgement on this occasion he did not allow the decision to diminish his respect for his old leader.

O'Neill's method of succession also put him greatly in the debt of the Chief Whip, William Craig, who had worked hard behind the scenes to help O'Neill's candidature. Craig at that time was a relatively unknown and struggling lawyer in search of a political patron. His support for O'Neill became the basis of a close relationship during which Craig received rapid promotion, making him one of the most powerful and controversial figures in Irish politics. For over five years, 1963 to 1968, these two oddly contrasting men were bound to each other in a political marriage which was mutually destructive and which caused great difficulties for the community they sought to serve. When they parted company they had done great damage to each other, and the Province faced the most ruinous crisis in its history.

But in 1963 William Craig was a key figure in the O'Neill bid for power and was much valued by his master. He managed to use the traditional 'soundings' system to the advantage of his candidate and used his influence inside the parliamentary party to secure support. As with Douglas-Home at Westminster, O'Neill got a reluctant majority from his backbenchers and was confirmed in office. Craig shared in the new Prime Minister's success and gained rapid promotion along with other O'Neill-ites. But the method of O'Neill's elevation remained a subject of controversy and led to demands for a change in the system of leadership selection; these demands had to be granted. Altogether, it was a difficult start for what was to prove a perilous premiership.

Faulkner shared the reservations which many felt about the new leader and showed early in the life of the new Government that he was uneasy about what had happened. In the proceedings of the House of Commons in the first year of O'Neill's term there were many allusions to the tension by members of the opposition, anxious to harry the new administration. On one occasion (29 October 1963) the following scene is recorded in Hansard:

MR FAULKNER: The Government are united. They are a Government which are working hard as a united team and going ahead under a young and vigorous Prime Minister. If I were not at one with the policies of the Government I would not for twenty-four hours be a member of that Government and from what I know of the Prime Minister if his team were not united he would not wish to lead it.

MR BLEAKLEY: Did the Minister support his election? Does he think he is the best man for the job?

MR DIAMOND: He is pasting over the cracks.

MR FAULKNER: Having said that as clearly as any man can say anything, let me say that I am wholeheartedly behind the Prime Minister. I could not say it any more clearly than I am. What does the hon. Member for Victoria want me to say? I am wholeheartedly behind the Prime Minister.

MR BLEAKLEY: Does the Minister think the Prime Minister is the best man for the job?

MR FAULKNER: I believe that this Government are a strong Government and in every aspect of their policy they are working together.

It was a superb exercise in evasion and the House knew it. A 'best Prime Minister we have' performance all over again. R. A. Butler could not have done better.

Later that day Tom Boyd, the Labour leader, continued the torture:

MR BOYD: Mr Faulkner has said that the Government are united. United in what? He has been challenged to say whether he stands loyally behind his present leader and so far he has not specifically said so.

MR FAULKNER: On a point of correction. The hon. Member for Pottinger has just made what I believe to be—I find it difficult to restrain my language—something which is not true. He says that I refused to say in this House that I was loyally behind the Prime Minister. I hope he will read Hansard and when does he will find—

MR BLEAKLEY: Does the Minister think the PM is the best man for the job?

MR FAULKNER: —the first thing I said was that this was a united Government and that I was solidly behind the Prime Minister. What the hon. Member said was a shameful thing to say.

MR BOYD: The Minister has ignored the specific terms of the challenge and I will now repeat it to him. Does he now pledge his loyalty to the Prime Minister, never mind whether the Government are united or not?

There was no answer from Faulkner—like the good hunting man he was, he knew when he was cornered and did not resist further. The Prime Minister, who was watching, undoubtedly took the point. As one observer noted at the time, O'Neill's lean and hungry look got leaner and hungrier as Faulkner refused to give the personal commitment which was required of his lieutenants. So it went on down the years—Faulkner ever anxious to defend the government in general, but never O'Neill in person. The Prime Minister was equally sparing in personal praise for his Minister of Commerce.

Even as early as 1966 O'Neill found grounds for suspicion. As he put it in a letter to Faulkner: 'I enclose a transcript of an interview which you gave from America, while I was struggling for my political life in 1966. You will see that you were specifically asked to say whether or not you supported me as Prime Minister and that you took refuge in ambiguities about government policy. Had you been willing to give straight answers to questions such as these on a number of occasions it would both have sustained me, and, I am sure, increased respect for you.' [31]

Perhaps O'Neill was being naïve here. It is hard to imagine either of these strong and divergent personalities ever expressing personal support for each other. Any alliance they achieved was based on mutual convenience rather than mutual respect.

O'Neill and Faulkner did, however, attempt to work together and an uneasy partnership developed for a while between them. During the process Faulkner emerged as second-in-command and made a valuable contribution to the government through his industrial activities. It was even suggested that O'Neill intended eventually to hand over to Faulkner, retiring early in order to make way for him. Faulkner, however, did not attach much importance to such possibilities—a view confirmed in 1969. So, as time went on, the two men drifted apart—O'Neill complaining of lack of personal support and Faulkner objecting to what he regarded as a presidential style of government at Stormont and an increasing alienation from the rank and file of the party. 'He never told you what he was doing': this was Faulkner's complaint about the leader.

It was a tragic fact that these two complex and talented men had an extraordinary low level of tolerance for each other. O'Neill was all that Faulkner was not and did not wish to be: Eton, the Guards and Anglican. Faulkner, for his part, was only 'in trade' as far as the landed aristocracy was concerned—someone who, in their eyes, did not know his proper place. The two men even disagreed on their attitude to their old leader. Faulkner was deeply loyal to Brookeborough and still regards him as 'one of Ulster's greatest leaders and a fine man to serve under'; O'Neill's subsequent comments on the veteran Unionist were devastating and deeply resented by the family and a wide spectrum of Ulster opinion. [32]

Indeed, O'Neill's aloofness cost him many friends and at times he could have done with some of Brookeborough's country charm. Unfortunately he was in many ways a prisoner of the aristocratic remoteness associated with the O'Neill line. It was at once his greatest asset and his heaviest liability—good for foreign consumption, but difficult to retail at home.

The personality problem was often illustrated when O'Neill was trying to establish better relationships with the Catholic population. With Roman Catholics, being an O'Neill was an initial advantage and it enabled the Prime Minister to make imaginative (by Unionist standards) gestures to the Catholic community on a scale never before attempted by a Unionist administration. Catholics welcomed the promised new relationships, and Charles Stewart, MP for Queen's University, spoke for many of his fellow Catholics when he congratulated the new government in a Commons speech in March 1963: 'It is pleasant to know that at long last we have here a Prime Minister of Northern Ireland, a person descended one way or another from Eoghan, son of Niall of the Nine Hostages, and that one of the great clans of Ulster is now represented well and truly in the chair of Prime Minister. Although he was educated at Eton, on which we commend him entirely, I only hope that his love of England will be exceeded by his love of Ireland.'

This welcome reflected opinion among Irish Catholics, North and South, and won the Premier support from quarters unaccustomed to voting Unionist. It was right for O'Neill to make the attempt and a great pity that more of his party had not made the move earlier. But O'Neill laboured under the difficulty of his clan: he moved among the Roman Catholic population like some ancient lord, anxious to do the decent thing by his tenants. By his own lights he tried hard (certainly harder than any previous Unionist leader) to address himself to the Catholic community, but he could not really make contact on mutually acceptable terms.

Indeed, when he did comment on the position of Roman Catholics in Northern Ireland, O'Neill could be revealingly offensive. In a widely quoted interview to the *Belfast Telegraph* (10 May 1969) he had this to say: 'It is frightfully hard to explain to Protestants that if you give Roman Catholics a good job and a good house, they will live like Protestants, because they will see neighbours with cars and television sets. They will refuse to have eighteen children; but if a Roman Catholic is jobless, and lives in the most ghastly hovel, he will rear eighteen children on national assistance. If you treat Roman Catholics with due consideration and kindness, they will live like Protestants in spite of the authoritative nature of their Church.'

As Conor Cruise O'Brien put it in a gentle but penetrating rebuke: 'It would have been even more "frightfully hard" to explain this to Catholics. Although these words were not spoken while O'Neill was still premier, the Olympian attitude which they express was perceptible and unhelpful to his cause.' [33]

O'Neill's Olympian attitude, resented among his Catholic countrymen, was also a factor which caused difficulty with Protestant colleagues and followers. In the sturdy Ulster farmer there is a resentment of regal airs and Lord of the Manor attitudes; something less lordly is demanded by those of Planter stock with strong Scottish Presbyterian traditions. O'Neill's style of government was easily misunderstood and led to disagreements which weakened support for some of his most important initiatives. Yet the style was to be expected. O'Neill was a clan leader without an estate. This deprivation was brought to an end in 1963 when, in a sense, the whole Province became an O'Neill domain once again. He ruled over it as a medieval baron who genuinely believed that he knew what was best for those who lived on the estate. He did manage for a while to become the most popular Ulsterman abroad and in a series of telling speeches and actions triggered off events in the Province which changed for all time the existing political mould. However, he never managed to win for himself the personal majority on which such high adventures must rest. Nor did he seem to realise that powerful personalities like Faulkner could not be ignored. This was a defect which soured his relations with a series of important colleagues. As Conservative MP, John Biggs-Davison, has noted: 'O'Neill failed, where less exalted, even less virtuous men may succeed, because in a democracy for a politician to fail in management and appeal is to fail as a statesman.' [34]

O'Neill's difficulties with his cabinet were increased by his tendency to avoid proper consultation on major political initiatives. Faulkner, as Deputy, particularly resented this and it set him farther apart from his leader.

The famous Lemass visit to Belfast in 1965 brought these tensions to a head. It was an imaginative move on O'Neill's part to invite the Prime Minister of the Republic on a first-ever official visit to Northern Ireland, and by local standards it was a revolutionary event. At last an official meeting between Northern and Southern premiers had taken place and for each of the participants it marked a new stage in their political development and in the relations between the states they represented.

For O'Neill, however, it brought internal party difficulties and though he got a vote of confidence in Parliament he had to face influential criticism which gained in strength as his opponents took advantage of the backlash opinion against the visit, generated among right-wing elements in his party.

In the Commons debate of 3 February 1965, veteran statesman Edmund Warnock, a former Attorney-General, spoke for many Unionists when he described the Prime Minister's decision to bring Mr Lemass to the North without the authority of cabinet backing as 'an unwarrantable assumption of personal dictatorship' and an invasion of 'the policy of collective responsibility'. Here, Warnock was pressing home an accusation which was to increase in frequency in the years ahead. He also accused the Premier of treating the parliamentary party with 'contemptuous indifference'.

O'Neill in reply rejected the accusations and insisted that there are occasions when a Prime Minister 'must judge the temper of the times and take a step forward on his own authority. If he has judged aright the sentiments of the country, Parliament will endorse his action. This is the secret of leadership'. It was a defiant answer on O'Neill's part and he got his endorsement; but many who voted for him must have questioned his 'secret of leadership' definition as they did so.

Faulkner, as a cabinet minister, remained silent in the debate, but shared in private the concern that in taking an independent line on such a vital issue the Prime Minister was setting a pace that the party organisation and circumstances in the country might not be able to sustain. In the event, the strongest support for the North/South détente came from outside the Unionist Party rather than from within; this itself was a warning of trouble ahead.

Soon after the Lemass visit there were tensions inside the Cabinet and among backbench MPs an 'O'Neill must go' campaign gained strength. Significantly, the dissident members turned to Faulkner for advice and on one occasion a rebellious group, accompanied by Harry West, Minister of Agriculture, visited his home to acquaint him with their views. O'Neill knew of these activities (Faulkner claims that he kept the Chief Whip informed of developments) and, naturally enough, deeply resented what was going on.

One other Cabinet dispute added to the coolness between Faulkner and O'Neill—the dismissal of Harry West from the government. In the summer of 1967 a bitter disagreement developed between the Prime Minister and his Minister of Agriculture over the purchase of some land in County Fermanagh. West, at that time a very popular and successful minister, had decided to buy the land in order to retain it in his family. But because of the interest of the county council in its purchase it was suggested that West should make certain that the business was conducted in a manner which would not embarrass him as a cabinet minister. Acting on legal advice, the Minister completed the purchase in accordance with what he regarded as proper standards.

O'Neill disagreed—and instead of delivering the verbal rebuke which some of his colleagues expected from him, he demanded the resignation of the minister. At first the public concluded that the land was the only issue, but in the debate that followed it became obvious that some members of the Unionist Party and of the opposition saw the incident as part of the personal power struggle going on inside the Cabinet.

O'Neill insisted that his only desire was to impose what he regarded as the necessary standards of behaviour required where there was a possible conflict between public duty and private interest. However, it soon became clear[35] that influential members of his Parliament were not prepared to support this interpretation of events and saw something more personal in the Prime Minister's action. Veteran Socialist Republican MP, Harry Diamond, no supporter of Mr West, was in no doubt and suggested that for a long time there had been a sustained campaign against the former Minister of Agriculture. He added, 'is he to be the first of a number who are likely to be dismissed because they took the wrong side during a recent conspiracy against the Prime Minister?'

Mr West himself was in no doubt about the motives of the Prime Minister. In a passionate defence of his position, he accused O'Neill of making unfair use of the whole incident to even up old scores: 'I deeply regret that the Prime Minister in his apparent desire to dispose of my services as a member of his administration should come to the Dispatch Box with charges which were not justified, quotations taken from letters completely out of context and erroneous and misleading allegations on my use of privileged knowledge. Is it any wonder that at this moment my faith in the dignity of mankind has been greatly shaken.'

In a dramatic intervention Lord Brookeborough rose to accept West's explanation and found it 'impossible to believe there was any dishonesty on his part'. He asked O'Neill to reconsider the matter and warned him that the whole of the County Fermanagh was 'up in arms' about his action.

Notwithstanding the doctrine of collective responsibility, Faulkner also came to the defence of the dismissed minister and publically disputed the Prime Ministei's judgement. He complained that reports on the media gave a quite unfair 'Impression of dishonest dealing' and, like Brookeborough, considered that there was no question of 'any dishonourable conduct'. Mr Diamond, in yet another contribution, was even more blunt. He concluded that the former minister had 'been framed' and saw the incident as another chapter in the 'so-called conspiracy against the Prime Minister'. In an allusion to the power of the O'Neill family 'that runs this Government and runs this state', Diamond warned that 'if one falls foul of them one will quickly lost his political head'. He considered that the dismissal of Harry West was 'a form of intimidation' and warned that 'the Minister of Commerce (Mr Faulkner) can rest assured that he will go the same way as the former Minister of Agriculture'.

The O'Neill/West controversy was a watershed in the relations of O'Neill with his parliamentary party and thereafter a split became ever more evident as cabinet colleagues began to watch each other warily. Many observers felt that there was truth in the quip attributed to one of the Prime Minister's friends on hearing of West's dismissal: 'That's one gone and there are two (Faulkner and Morgan) to go.' There is no doubt that the West dismissal raised objections which would have warned a more sensitive politician to take greater care. Instead, in the eyes of many Unionist Party members, O'Neill added insult to injury when a few days later he announced that cousin and fellow Etonian, Major James Chichester-Clarke, was to become the new Minister of Agriculture. Many gasped in surprise—but the O'Neill retinue simply asked: 'Who else?'

The treatment of Harry West had a profound effect on Faulkner. Ever after he regarded the incident as evidence of the PM's lack of judgement and his inability to hold the party together. He also took Mr Diamond's warning to heart and seemed to feel that O'Neill would pursue him as relentlessly as he had other rivals. So, in the critical years of 1967–69 these two key figures in Ulster politics drifted further apart and were unable to achieve a real working partnership. Equally, Harry West was lost to government service, and others were to follow. At a crucial time in Ulster politics when influential people should have been pulling in unison for the public good they were drifting apart. A powerful figure was needed to draw them together; the massive presence of Morris May was missed.

From 1967 relations between Faulkner and O'Neill were increasingly wary. Faulkner continued to make a success of the Ministry of Commerce and jobs and new industries flowed to the Province. O'Neill, for his part, was increasingly swept along by the speed of events into a situation which gradually got out of control. By the beginning of 1969 Faulkner felt he could go no further. He complained that O'Neill had become more and more remote and was incapable of giving decisive leadership; in turn, O'Neill questioned Faulkner's personal loyalty. It was the old friction between them all over again. When the break came in January 1969 it was obvious that each had had more than enough of the other. The mutual disenchantment is clear in the resignation letters which passed between them. Faulkner wrote:

'The essential need is strong government capable of either: 1, gaining the confidence of the Unionist Party for a change of policy and introducing on its own initiative adult suffrage in the local government franchise—which I personally believe to be the right course; or 2, resisting the pressures being brought to bear upon the Government. In either case, law and order must be enforced.

This administration falls down on both the alternatives I have mentioned.'

This short extract from a brief resignation letter was a severe criticism of the O'Neill administration on the essential count of 'strong government'. Many, however, who noted Faulkner's concern for local government voting reform, wished that he had displayed a more enlightened attitude in his years as Minister of Home Affairs. O'Neill's reply to this letter denied the charge of weak government and suggested that if Faulkner had given 'the loyalty and support which a Prime Minister has the right to expect from his Deputy, some of the so-called crises might never have arisen'.

Faulkner responded by insisting that he had always given full support: 'I am hurt by your reference to lack of support during my period of office. There is much I could say, but I would prefer not to indulge in recrimination.' O'Neill, in yet another long and public reply, returned to the charge of personal disloyalty and produced quotations taken from his rival's speeches down the years which, he believed, illustrated his case.

Faulkner, never much given to personal recriminations, did not reply, but the public exchanges showed that as far back as 1966 deep-seated difficulties had arisen between the two Unionist leaders. Mutual trust and respect were lacking between them. It was an undignified ending to a partnership which might have led to great things if each had been able to give and take a little more. Unfortunately for Ulster, the giving and the taking called for sacrifices in areas of personality and basic philosophy in which neither was willing to give way.

O'Neill in his autobiography revealed a dislike for Faulkner which was considerable and personal. Faulkner, who usually ignores personal attacks, has so far made little public comment on the former Prime Minister, but it seems certain that his opinion when it comes will be no less scathing than that passed by Lord O'Neill on his old leader, Lord Brookeborough.

With the departure of Faulkner and William Morgan from office, O'Neill's government began to break up, as the Prime Minister had to rely more and more on people with little grass-roots appeal. Eventually in 1969 the famous 'Crossroads' election was called, in which the Prime Minister made a determined defence of his policies. Britain and the world were most impressed, but, again, O'Neill was speaking over the heads of Ulster people who for generations had been taught by the Unionist Party to reject such liberal sentiments; worse still, his own party had yet to be converted to the philosophy he was propounding. The effort to preserve the unity of that party doomed to failure the eloquent appeal for reconciliation made in election '69. Roman Catholics, sensing the ambiguity in O'Neill's position, drew their own conclusion and, as he mournfully noted later, they withheld the massive Province-wide support which he expected and needed. He won the election, but knew that he had lost the battle; even in his own seat of Bannside his chief tormentor, Ian Paisley, came a close second.

Fifty miles away in East Down Faulkner fought off a traditional nationalist challenge, along with that of an O'Neillite Unionist, to gain yet another substantial victory. From then on he was clearly in a much stronger position within the party than the Prime Minister. What everyone had been forecasting for twenty years was now coming to pass—the leadership of Northern Ireland was about to move from the control of the landed aristocracy into the hands of one who belonged to a newer and more representative (though still staunchly conservative) social group.

But before the crown was transferred finally, O'Neill was able to strike one more blow. Faulkner was opposed by Chichester-Clarke in the contest for the premiership. At first, few took the challenge seriously, but an alliance of the county families and the new Unionists O'Neill had brought into the party was formed against Faulkner. It was a disastrous success: Faulkner was beaten in the contest by one vote. O'Neill had used his own vital vote against his old foe. As he was to put it later on: 'I couldn't have brought myself to vote for the man who had been trying to bring me down for six years. It was as simple as that.' [36] Perhaps; but as a parting shot it was a poor contribution to a people who, facing the most terrible crisis in their history, desperately needed a strong leader.

Chichester-Clarke staggered on manfully for twenty-two months, comprehending little and enjoying nothing of the political disaster in which he was involved. Faulkner won a great deal of respect in standing by the failing Prime Minister during this period and, as Minister of Development, piloted a major local government reform programme through a parliament that was falling apart for want of a new dynamic.

In March 1971 Chichester-Clarke at last felt able to resign with honour. With a sigh of relief he returned to the gentler cares of his extensive farm lands; he was given a kindly, but relieved, farewell by the Province.

Most people now agreed that Faulkner's turn had come and even those who disagreed with his views were resigned to what seemed inevitable; only William Craig felt bold enough to offer himself as an alternative. He received four votes from the parliamentary party. At last the Member for East Down had entered into the inheritance which on two occasions had eluded him. He can hardly have been surprised at his elevation, but, like many before him, he must have felt it more comfortable to journey hopefully than to arrive in Ulster's top post in 1971. When he did arrive time was running out for the system over which he was asked to preside. Apt, indeed, was the description applied to him at the time: the Prime Minister who came too late.

CHAPTER SEVEN

Year at the Top

Terence O'Neill's career was one of frustrated promise, during which he had created for Ulster people their own revolution of rising expectations; unfortunately, he was not able to satisfy the hopes he had raised. But in his outline of new frontiers he had begun to inscribe a political invoice for the future. Ironically, it was his greatest rival who faced up to the infinitely more difficult task of expanding the order and delivering the goods.

When Faulkner became Prime Minister in March 1971, he took over at a desperate moment in the life of the Province, but in a typical display of determination he began to grasp whatever advantages were available in the new situation. He had waited a long time for the premiership and, as with others who had achieved this ambition, the attitudes adopted in the climb to the top began to give way to a political life-style needed to consolidate the position reached and designed to make full use of the new opportunities.

Public opinion was on the side of the new Prime Minister in 1971. Many had sympathised with him when he had been outvoted by Chichester-Clarke's supporters in 1969 and the sympathy had grown as, in the role of Deputy Prime Minister, he had more and more shouldered the full burden of leadership. His succession, when it came, seemed to many to be overdue, and to most it was a just reward for years of persistent application.

But though the public gave Faulkner a ready welcome the professional politicians were more cautious. From Social Democratic Labour Party leader, Mr Gerry Fitt, came the charge that the new government lacked 'credibility'. Mr John Hume agreed with this and accused Faulkner of being party to 'a pretence and charade of democracy'. The new Premier fared no better at the hands of right-wing Unionists. Mr Paisley's *Protestant Telegraph* did not deny that the new man was a 'competent and efficient Parliamentarian' but foresaw that he would 'prove demanding and dictatorial'. The paper believed that while the support of 'mindless backbenchers' had been secured, he would have "no volume of support" among the grass-roots loyalists'. While the nationalists may have been suspicious of Faulkner for his distant past, for loyalists it was recent history that mattered most: 'We remember him for his pushing through the reform programme, including the Housing Executive Bill. We remember him for his enthusiasm for cross-border talks. We know that he has had secret talks with Cardinal Conway. That should please the Orange brethren. We know of his business interests in the South of Ireland. Faulkner's declared policies are but the sugar coating of a bitter pill, and during the next few weeks the real, the aggressive, the dictatorial Faulkner will emerge, but he could be Ulster's shortest reigning Prime Minister, as we will not tolerate any further erosion of our standards and principles.' [37] Buffeted equally by both sides, not for the first time, Faulkner must have thought 'you cannot win!'

But the opinion of the politicians was not representative and most Ulster people were prepared to give the new administration a fair trial. Many people also realised that time was running out for the Province and agreed with those who believed that a 'last chance' Prime Minister had arrived.

Very soon, however, the new premier was showing his outstanding resilience and his ability to fight his way out of a difficult corner. Everything began to seem possible as he began to break entirely new ground—new by the conservative standards associated with traditional Unionist leadership.

Signs of a special brand of Faulkner Unionism appeared in his approach to cabinet building. Unlike his predecessors, he was prepared to step outside the usual framework of Ulster politics. Realising that official Unionist custom and practice was no longer sufficient for the immediate crisis, Faulkner declared that in creating his government he sought to develop 'not a rigid or doctrinaire administration representative of any single opinion or outlook, but a broadly-based government, which brings together men who stand united in the interests of the country'. In the new Cabinet the broadest possible spectrum of Unionism was represented. Harry West, dropped by O'Neill, returned to his beloved Ministry of Agriculture (in which he rapidly became immersed, doing an excellent job for the farmers and seemingly happy to leave aside other political activities), Robin Baillie (a Bow Group type, who a few years later joined the Alliance Party) came in as Minister of Commerce and as a strong supporter of the EEC. Other members who represented various shades of Unionism joined the new team. By all accounts it was a shrewd balance, though, at the same time, it attracted a cross-section of reservations.

But Faulkner was not content to confine his team to members of the Unionist Party. Down the years his party had been criticised for its monopoly of power. No prime minister to date had sought to shift the balance. Faulkner decided to innovate. In a surprise move, he sought the assistance of his political opponents, the Labour Party. A member of the Northern Ireland Labour Party (the present writer) was invited to become Minister of Community Relations in the new government and to accept a seat in the Cabinet.

Faulkner's approach in making this appointment was typical of his workmanlike style. As is recorded elsewhere,[38] the day had started as usual in teaching at the Methodist College, Belfast. It was interrupted by a telephone call from Robert Ramsey, the Prime Minister's Secretary. Could I come to Stormont Castle at 10.15 a.m.? Mr Faulkner had some important business to discuss. There was, in fact, nothing unusual about such a call. Peace planning often involved such visits, and our liberal headmaster, A. S. Worrall, granted generous leave. But this time it was different. The Prime Minister came to the point straight away. He had been asked by the Governor to form a new government and was anxious to construct a Cabinet which would have broadly-based community support. The country must be got going again, the reform programme had to be carried through, and other reforms would follow as stability was established. The time had come for a united effort.

I was not a Member of Parliament, but here again there was no problem. I could be sworn in as a Privy Councillor and on that basis would be able to join the Cabinet for at least the six-month period which would then become constitutionally possible. Would I join on this basis as Minister of Community Relations to do the job as I thought fit? There would be no strings and no interference with my labour or trade union membership or obligations (undertakings honoured at all times). Could I give my answer by one o'clock?

In that manner Brian Faulkner made his offer and created a new pattern for inter-party appointments to government in Northern Ireland. At a luncheon later in the day, attended by Jim Callaghan (who that evening gave his generous support on TV), I indicated my acceptance of the offer. A new Minister of Community Relations had been appointed to the Northern Ireland Government and a first-ever member of the Labour Party had been admitted to the Cabinet of the Province.

The decision to serve in Faulkner's government was, initially, a lonely one. In 1971 the concept of community government in Northern Ireland was new and was not popular in any of the major political parties in Parliament. But I had no doubts; since 1969 the erosion of the social and political structure indicated all too clearly that political tribalism based on sectarian confrontation had had its day—that some form of community power-sharing (and, more important, responsibility sharing) would have to take its place. Someday, somehow, a start had to be made.

Subsequent developments have confirmed this judgement. But in 1971 Faulkner was ahead of his time in making a move in the direction of power-sharing, however tentative it was. By having the courage to make the offer and in finding a positive response from a representative of the Labour movement the Premier had made a first contribution to the concept of partnership in government. He had created a precedent which made future constitutional thinking along similar lines easier to develop. Nor was the offer a once-for-all gesture on Faulkner's part. By his decision later in 1971 to appoint Dr G. B. Newe, a leading Roman Catholic layman, to his Cabinet he showed that he was willing, in practice, to pursue the idea earlier and more effectively than any other Unionist leader. On another occasion he also approached a leading trade union official (another non-Unionist) to join the government.

In March 1971, Faulkner, never inclined to produce a theory to explain his actions, gave no indication that he was deliberately experimenting with new forms of government, but it was a sound instinct that made him aware of the need to reach out for assistance beyond the Ulster Unionist Party. Towards the end of his premiership he began to talk more openly about his hopes for a broadening of the base of power and for a party membership that was non-sectarian. As he put it to the Commons (3 November 1971): 'I look forward to the day when my Unionist colleagues on this Front Bench will be Protestant and Catholic, and no one will even think it worthy of comment. Neither Unionist nor Ulster will survive in the long run if we take any other course.'

Faulkner proved an easy man with whom to work. He interfered little, if at all, in the work of individual departments, though, with his remarkable memory and grasp for detail, he was aware of what his ministers were doing. At cabinet meetings he was more of an Attlee than a Churchill in approach. He gave no long monologues; he let every member have a fair say, and at the end gave a brisk summing-up and a firm indication of what was the will of the meeting. Usually, in fact, ministers had their way in the affairs of their own department, but when disagreement did emerge he made sure that a definite decision was recorded and that no loose ends were left lying about. Nor were there any favourites among his ministers, and Cabinet sub-committees were not encouraged to proliferate or to take important decisions away from the full Cabinet.

Faulkner also gave his ministers a very free rein in their extra-mural activities. With such a mixed group perhaps this was just as well. Not infrequently, however, the speeches of one member gave offence to some other. When such situations arose he merely mentioned the fact and left it to the good sense of the members concerned to iron out their differences. On one occasion, when his Labour Minister of Community Relations headed the local trade union May Day parade, some Cabinet colleagues expressed their annoyance. Faulkner, when the subject was brought up, merely smiled and reminded those concerned that they too were active marchers—but at local Orange gatherings! He then went on to congratulate his Minister on a successful march. Lord Grey, the Governor, more puckishly, at a reception for Privy Councillors that evening, asked if the Minister's feet were sore after his splendid effort.

On yet another occasion when the same Minister disturbed local Unionist MPs by calling for a referendum on the Common Market the Prime Minister, when asked if his approval for the speech had been sought, gave the reply: 'No, Sir. I do not expect any of my colleagues to submit their public speeches to me for prior approval.' Nor did he. Colleagues were trusted and the trust was respected.

But on security policy Faulkner kept a very watchful and private eye. He decided to assume the Home Affairs portfolio himself and established a new security branch which reported to him personally. Members of the Cabinet often expressed the feeling that they were not closely enough involved with this aspect of policy nor sufficiently consulted. Even 'hawkish' Minister of State, John Taylor, was given little opportunity to play a leading role in security and was expected to specialise in the more routine aspects of the Ministry's work. In fairness to Faulkner, he felt that the security issue was paramount and should not have to compete for room on the always crowded cabinet agenda; but there is also no doubt that his total identification with security was a deliberate choice and at no time did he give the impression that he wished it otherwise. On the contrary, he seemed positively to welcome the widely held belief that he was 'Mr Security' in Northern Ireland. This was a decision which proved damaging in other areas of his policy development.

The main aspects of Faulkner's initial approach to policy matters were given in the Debate on the Address in March 1971. In the main it was a typically businesslike speech, linking prosperity and security and promising 'peace and stability and the full and speedy implementation of the progressive social and economic policies to which the administration is pledged'. His words were cautiously received, but most Members spent their time examining the implication of the Prime Minister's choice of team. The SDLP, in particular, expressed doubts about the inclusion of Harry West and found little good to say about his other innovations. They were joined by Ian Paisley who regarded the combination as 'a bag of dolly-mixtures'.

However, if the House had been less anxious to score points they would have paid special attention to two related themes which the Premier had slipped into the general social and economic content of his remarks (new ideas often appeared this way—a line or word casually inserted becoming the first step in a radical new departure). During an otherwise flat speech Faulkner took up the theme of inter-communal relations and stressed his determination to make 'no distinction between Protestant and Roman Catholic, between Unionist and anti-Partitionist'. His aim would be 'to serve all the people of Northern Ireland'. In subsequent months this theme became a major element in many official speeches and statements.

Faulkner's second new theme concerned relations inside Parliament. Here he stressed that Parliament belonged to all the Members (a far cry from the old-fashioned Unionist Party days of 'a Protestant Parliament for a Protestant people'), and, in particular, he saw a key role for the Opposition. He offered to have discussions with Mr Fitt, leader of the largest opposition group, so as to enable the House to reach an agreed approach on matters of common concern. Little attention was paid to these overtures, but seeds were being sown which would blossom at the Darlington and Sunningdale conferences some months and many crises later. The appeal was rounded-off with the hope, expressed so consistently down the years, that the government 'should be judged on their record, on what they actually do, rather than on fanciful speculation about what they might do'.

Unfortunately Faulkner did not have much time in his year of office to accumulate many legislative achievements, but even in the short time available a new framework of ideas was discernible. While developing this framework he did not take up a doctrinaire position, either Unionist or Conservative, and he managed to get Cabinet agreement for projects which, in any other period in the history of the Province, might well have caused a split in the administration. Indeed, very rarely did the Cabinet get into doctrinal dispute; the times were too pressing for other than practical propositions.

In the field of industry, for example, when it was decided to make the government a major shareholder in the local ship-building firm of Harland and Wolff, no objections were raised. Equally, there was agreement when the government decided to reject Mr Heath's proposal for the Industrial Relations Act. Even on such a politically sensitive point as this, no difficulty arose: the Act was not introduced in the Province but, instead, it was announced that 'independent and prudent initiatives' (a nice thrust at the British Conservative Government's attitude to industrial relations) would be pursued in collaboration with the CBI and the Irish Congress of Trade Unions 'to mobilise the knowledge and experience of both sides of industry in Northern Ireland to help formulate the most harmonious and effective system of industrial relations'. This was later described in an official statement as an act of faith by the government in the goodwill, the objectivity and the sense of public responsibility of both employers and unions.

At a time when Mr Heath was insisting on a tough anti-union line, this was a strong assertion of local independence and showed Faulkner's determination to maintain a local stance in a policy area where he felt he was a greater expert than the leader of the British Conservative Party. Subsequent events proved him correct in his judgement. While Britain reeled under industrial disputes Northern Ireland, in marked contrast, produced a system of employer/union relations which has given the region one of the best industrial peace records in western Europe. So good, indeed, is the degree of co-operation between unions and government in Northern Ireland that one of the first public relations exercises of the new Executive was to take half-page advertisements in the national press in which Mr William Blease, Regional Secretary of the Irish Congress of Trade Unions in Northern Ireland, was pictured making a call for new business. His language tells much about the special industrial conditions of the region: 'Ours is no doctrinaire approach. Certainly we are committed to achieving full employment and a higher standard of living for all our people. However, we realise that the right industrial conditions have to be created if new manufacturing investment is to be attracted to Northern Ireland and we understand full well that profitability has to be assured if new industry is to expand and so to create further employment. We promise a sane approach to industrial relations. A fair deal by employers for our members guarantees a fair deal for employers from the Trade Union movement in Northern Ireland. Anyone creating new jobs through manufacture in Northern Ireland can expect maximum co-operation and help from us'.

Ulster had got by happily, indeed, without the Industrial Relations Act.

In another sensitive area of industrial affairs, fair employment policies, Faulkner proved a pioneer. Catholics had long argued that they were discriminated against where job allocation was concerned. The new Prime Minister became the first Unionist to legislate against the practice. A law was passed debarring from public contracts any firm which practised any form of religious discrimination in the performance of the contract. This move was an important lead to the rest of industry and the private sector immediately took steps to introduce similar safeguards.

Catholic objections were also met in the long-standing dispute over the finances of the Mater Hospital in Belfast. Since the inception of the welfare state this great hospital, owned by the Roman Catholic Church, had been excluded from state financial help. As a result, the hospital had built up huge debts as it continued to serve the medical needs of the whole community on a voluntary basis. Efforts down the years to bring the hospital into the state scheme had failed and in some respects the argument had degenerated into a tortuous administrative tangle. There were also sectarian overtones to the dispute which gave great offence to the Catholic population as they geared their local charities to strenuous fund-raising activities. Many Protestants shared the sense of scandal and felt that some relief ought to be given.

Once again, the Prime Minister was anxious to finalise an agreement. He actively encouraged the negotiations which his Minister of Health and loyal supporter, William Fitzsimmons, was conducting. These went well and on 1 December 1971, at a time of acute communal crisis, the Minister was able to inform the House that an agreement had been reached between the government and the Mater Infirmorum Hospital for the transfer of the hospital to the hospital service on mutually acceptable terms. It was the result of several years of patient negotiation and the event deserved wider publicity than it got. A few years earlier the agreement would have ranked as front-page material and as the mark of an enlightened administration, but in the mood of late 1971 it could not compete with more sombre news.

It was, in fact, Faulkner's misfortune that some of his most liberal initiatives had to be undertaken at a time when, inevitably, they were overshadowed by community tensions of greater public concern. Such, in particular, became the fate of his greatest initiative—the offer of a new system of government at Stormont based on inter-party committees of the House of Commons.

This offer was made in the middle of a remarkable speech delivered on the afternoon of 22 June 1971. The speech marked a turning point in Faulkner's thinking and spelt out in great detail the new philosophy at which he had hinted in his March speech on the Address. The occasion was well chosen. It was the fiftieth anniversary of the opening of the first Parliament of Northern Ireland. Ulster people, despite their troubles, were in festive mood and, Protestant and Catholic together, were aware that in fifty years they had established something of a common destiny. A Province-wide Festival was taking place and even the bombers left the colourful exhibitions halls and community events alone. With the aid of the poets, painters and playwrights of the Province, Planter and Gael for a few Golden Jubilee weeks were made to realise with a shy surprise that there was, deep down, a common heritage to be enjoyed and explored together.

Much of this sense of discovery was reflected in the Prime Minister's speech to the Commons. After pointing briefly to what he described as 'the most comprehensive programme of structural and other changes ever undertaken in Northern Ireland' he left the 'bricks and mortar' of progress and proceeded to startle the House by turning to questions concerning the fundamental nature of the Ulster community. With a reminder that all sides had fallen short in the past half-century, he proceeded to proclaim his faith in the possibility of a United Ulster where no false distinction would be drawn on the basis of religion or political affiliation. He frankly admitted his own mistakes and those of his party and suggested that the time had come for everyone to make a new start. He challenged the members to follow him in an entirely new effort to 'summon up new reserves of generosity and imagination' without which the Province could not progress, and went on to point out the possibilities inherent in the regional institutions of Northern Ireland, provided they could lay aside the inter-communal exchanges which had become 'increasingly bitter and sterile'.

Faulkner then proposed to a startled and increasingly rapt House that the government would give a new lead which would enable all—Protestant and Catholic together—to participate more fully in the work of government. He offered to establish a system of functional committees of the House in which some of the most powerful posts of Chairman would go to members of the opposition. These committees would be able to contribute to policy formation and would probe the executive functions of ministries and other agencies of government. All committees would be properly serviced and special allowances would be paid to members involved. In this way, he suggested, government and opposition alike would be involved more closely in the running of the state. He hoped that such a system would eliminate some of the inevitable frustrations and tensions associated with permanent opposition.

In the Northern Ireland setting such proposals constituted a fundamental shift in policy and the statement was regarded as such by politicians and public alike.

But more was to follow. Faulkner also took up a point which he had mentioned in passing in an earlier speech to the House—inter-party discussions. The times were serious and he believed that partisan conflict must be excluded as far as possible from the political arena. He did not believe that the aspirations of members on either side were as far apart as public speech-making might suggest. He wondered, therefore, if the needs of the country did not justify a serious attempt 'to bring the various political interests represented together for frank and wide-ranging discussions'. His conditions for such discussions revealed the new dimension in which he was working. There would have to be a full spectrum of views; talks would be open-ended; and while constitutional changes would not be on the agenda neither would any of the participants be expected 'in any way to derogate' from nationalist policies. He concluded by suggesting that the central purpose of the discussions should concern the common ground of restoring peace and stability and resuming social and economic advantages.

In the context of his time and party affiliation, Faulkner had made a remarkable gesture. Even his most severe critics recognised the magnitude of what he was saying and his proposals were listened to without interruption. When he had finished the 'Hear, hears' in the House were many-sided and enthusiastic. It was a key-note occasion and members recognised it as such.

From Mr Fitt, Leader of the Opposition, came a welcome for the promise 'to try new projects and to take a different line from that taken over the past fifty years'. He promised that if the Prime Minister put his words into action then he would have the co-operation of the opposition. The Labour spokesman, Mr Simpson, regarded the contribution as 'a very brilliant speech' and welcomed the 'genuine desire to share Parliamentary responsibility with the Opposition'. He promised the full support of the Labour movement. Mr Currie, a Catholic Member, and one of the strongest critics of the government, had no doubts either. For him, the debate had been one of the best of its kind since coming to the House: 'The Prime Minister is well aware that it is not very often I compliment him in public, or in private for that matter, but I intend to do so on this occasion. I think it was his contribution to this debate which encouraged other Members to contribute good speeches. He raised the tone of the debate and the result was that a number of other Members attempted to do the same thing.' Currie also promised that his side would be prepared to play a part in the House, as of right: 'We do not need to be invited to play our part. We are prepared to do so as Members of this House. We recognise what the Prime Minister asked us to recognise, namely that participation involves accepting burdens as well as enjoying advantages. We are quite prepared to accept those burdens.'

All that was needed to make Faulkner's triumph complete was a word of congratulation from Mr Paddy Devlin, for long his most turbulent opponent, and who a few months earlier had described him as a 'shrewd, cunning politician'. Devlin, too, had been won over and was generous in his tribute: 'Let me turn to the Prime Minister's proposals. I am quite surprised he made them. I had thought that like a lot of other people, he was discouraged and that his efforts would begin to tail off. I am pleased to welcome the proposals in the speech. They showed plenty of imagination. It was his best hour since I came into the House. If the promise that is contained in those proposals is implemented we will possibly get over the bad period towards which we are heading as a result of trouble on the streets. The Prime Minister has given hon. Members, and indirectly those outside, an opportunity to share in decision-making on a far greater scale than up to now.' When Faulkner came to reply to the debate he was visibly moved by the volume of praise which his new approach had evoked. Altogether, it was a new experience and one he could not fail to notice. He had released new ideas on to the local political scene and had discovered that his opponents were willing to listen; he had also discovered that beyond the bounds of traditional Unionism there was undiscovered country which was attractive to explore. He had begun to sense a new dimension; the Ulster Unionist was beginning to give way to the United Ulsterman. It was an hour of unusual glory; he basked deservedly in it.

But if June 1971 was Faulkner's finest moment in the House it was also the prelude to his most difficult period of trial and isolation. Increased violence on the streets of Northern Ireland in the summer of 1971 eroded political trust and soon all effective dialogue ended. In July the SDLP decided to intensify their campaign against Stormont and withdrew from the assembly by setting up a rival body of their own. The grand design for the future of government machinery in the Province got lost in the bitterness which followed. In the long hot summer the people of Northern Ireland, and the politicians with them, gradually lost sight of new schemes for government as they tried desperately to maintain any form of government at all in the face of a terrorist campaign which threatened the whole fabric of their lives. For most, the issues were too stark to allow time for erudite political discussion—survival was now the order of the hour. But the ideas enunciated by Faulkner had been good; their time was coming; in more opportune circumstances they would reassert themselves.

Faulkner's disappointment at the collapse of his plans was great and obvious. When Stormont resumed after the summer recess, emptied of its Catholic Members, the hopes of June seemed several light years away. A transformation had taken place and all were affected by the changed mood. With one sentence—'I do not think it is overstating matters to say that we rose for the summer recess in an atmosphere of caution and guarded optimism'—he alluded to the great moment in June and then proceeded grimly to the security problem which, in the remaining months of premiership, increasingly dominated his every thought and action. More and more he began to prepare for the Doomsday position which, he believed, was fast approaching.

Cabinet colleagues saw less and less of the Prime Minister as during the long hot summer of 1971 he became more and more absorbed by the problems of the security situation. During these weeks the pressure from bomb and bullet increased and Northern Ireland's political institutions tottered under the strain. At last, in August, Faulkner decided that a 'Doomsday position was apparent'. At that point he reached for the most controversial of all security weapons—internment.

In a matter of weeks after offering the concept of a United Ulster he was taking a course diametrically opposed to all he had been trying to say. Undoubtedly the pressures were great, but the miscalculation was massive in its implications. In resorting to internment Faulkner had made his greatest mistake; he was now about to learn his greatest lesson.

CHAPTER EIGHT

Internment—Miscalculation Supreme

Internment without trial is no new thing in Ireland, North or South, and politicians from most parties have from time to time supported the procedure. Indeed, when it has been used by the Dublin government internment has often been accompanied by other punitive measures of the utmost severity.

But in the North—unlike the South—the weapon has always had a sectarian edge to it, which has added greatly to its communal unacceptability. In the twenties, and again in the fifties, it was used regularly by the Northern Ireland Ministry of Home Affairs; as a result the Special Powers Act became one of the most controversial measures separating Protestant from Catholic.

And because the Unionist Party was Protestant and because, almost without exception, the internees came from the Roman Catholic community, the Catholic population came to regard internment as a legal insult directed solely at their community and as an intolerable example of the 'two people' tribal theory operating in the Province. Protestants, for the most part not particularly enthusiastic about the Special Powers Act, tended to regard it as a necessary evil, to be used to defend the Province against armed attacks on the lives and property of Northern Ireland citizens.

During the post-war period, tension eased in Northern Ireland as memories of earlier passions faded and as the Province benefited from welfare state legislation. Important differences still remained, but a sense of community oneness was emerging and the many who subscribed to the new view of things no longer saw themselves as belonging to neat 'Orange' or 'Green' categories—new blends were being arranged. Indeed, no longer was it even possible to tell a man's religion by his attitude to the border issue. As several independent surveys revealed, very considerable numbers of Catholics and anti-Unionist Party Protestants favoured British citizenship. There was in fact, in the 1950s and 1960s evidence of a considerable third force in the Ulster community—the concept of a united Province was beginning to challenge the more traditional United Ireland or divided Ulster alternatives.

As one of Ireland's leading Church thinkers, Dr Cathal Daly, Roman Catholic Bishop of Ardagh and Clonmacnois, has remarked about the outbreak of physical violence in the North: 'The tragedy is that the incipient growth of understanding and mutual acceptance which marked the ten years up to August 1969 has now been blighted by the frost of violence'.[40]

In such a situation of increasing understanding and mutual acceptance between Catholic and Protestant in post-war Northern Ireland, the Special Powers Act found even less support and when in the early 1960s it fell into disuse few people really mourned its departure; though still on the Statute Book, it had been effectively repealed by public opinion.

Faulkner was less certain of this repeal. During his period as Minister of Home Affairs he had taken over the internment policy of his predecessors and became convinced that the Special Powers Act was necessary for the security operations of his department. During his period in office the terrorist campaign of the fifties came to an end and his Unionist public gave him the credit for the cessation. Ever after, he remained convinced that he knew how to handle the IRA.

When he became Prime Minister in 1971 his interest in security was undiminished as he assumed control. He shared the responsibility with no other minister and made sure of his monopoly by combining the office of Prime Minister with that of Home Affairs. This was a considerable double burden to shoulder—politically it involved him in situations which hampered the more embracing community role he needed to develop as leader of the Province.

No doubt he recognised the need to use the powers of the

Home Affairs Ministry with discretion—indeed, there is evidence that he was unwilling to allow even his closest associates to share his influence on security matters. Politicians who worked for his Ministry, for instance, had to be content with coping with road traffic regulations and other such domestic activities of Home Affairs.

It is also clear that Faulkner was anxious to use internment only as a last resort. He was pressed continually in Cabinet and Parliament to use his powers of detention but he insisted on having sole personal responsibility in the matter and indicated that he would only move when there were 'clear security reasons' for doing so. A 'Doomsday situation', as he often put it, was what would persuade him to move.

What he never seemed to realise was that in such a sensitive area as internment there were implications which went well beyond purely security reasons. And because he depended heavily on the military and civil service for advice he was unlikely to be kept aware of those aspects which were important to Cabinet colleagues involved in the development of enterprises needing community co-operation.

Faulkner was convinced that his 'Doomsday situation' was appearing by the middle of 1971. For some months there had been a sharp escalation in violence and in July bomb attacks were taking place at the rate of three a day (in 1971 there were over a thousand explosions in the Province). Casualties were heavy (38 killed between January and August) and many hundreds injured. In addition, confidential reports were warning of a danger to water and electricity supplies as bombing attacks became more co-ordinated. There were also reports of foreign-based organisations aiding terrorist groupings.

Even the military were alarmed at the new escalation. Sir Harry Tuzo, G.O.C. Northern Ireland, warned: 'I doubt if there is anybody who is now raising their voice at the possibility of internment can really feel surprised or aggrieved if it were introduced after the chain of outrages which have occurred and which they appear to condone. Obviously if the kind of indiscriminate and utterly brutal action being perpetuated by the IRA were to continue they should not be surprised if this type of measure has to be introduced to protect the community.' [41]

On top of the security situation there was a catastrophic political deterioration. In July the SDLP decided to withdraw from the Stormont Parliament and to set up a rival assembly of their own. This, coming after the warm reception to his June proposals for parliamentary participation, greatly disappointed Faulkner and he promptly accused them of giving in to the 'hard men of Republicanism' who he claimed had made it clear to the SDLP that they were expected not to play a part at Stormont—however constructive a part they were offered—but to tear it down.' [42]

With the apparent failure of his political initiatives Faulkner became more absorbed by security problems. The 'indiscriminate and brutal activities' castigated by Tuzo did continue and on the 9 August 1971 the Prime Minister of Northern Ireland announced that internment had become necessary because 'no major alternative means of bringing the situation under control could be recommended by the security forces'. It was, as he put it, a 'very grave decision' taken 'in the light of the security advice and after consultation with Mr Heath and senior members of the United Kingdom Government'.

It was also a very lonely decision and deliberately so. Faulkner trusted his own judgement on security matters and was reluctant to discuss details in any meaningful way with his cabinet colleagues. Rarely was the whole Cabinet given an opportunity to have a full-scale discussion on the subject. Security had indeed been the last item on the agenda at a July meeting before leaving for the holidays, but even at this late stage there was no indication of a new move. Members were given the usual instructions to be available should they be needed during the summer vacation but nothing more as they dispersed for the traditional holiday period.

Even the Minister of Community Relations who would be likely to have a special concern with such a sensitive subject was not consulted. The first the Minister heard of the decision was a BBC report while on a touring holiday in Cornwall—at, of all places, Lands End! The same Minister had been in daily telephone contact with his Permanent Secretary in Belfast, but his department had received no prior warning of the event.

Such was the secrecy of the Prime Minister on security matters—his confidants were military and civil service personnel.

The internment operation when it did come in the early hours of 9 August 1971 was swift and spectacular. At 4.30 a.m. the army moved in on a Province-wide operation. Within an hour 300 men had been removed from their homes to the specially prepared troopship Maidstone, which was to become a prison-ship until Long Kesh camp was available.

A few hours later the world heard Brian Faulkner's announcement:

'I have had to conclude that the ordinary law cannot deal comprehensively or quickly enough with such ruthless viciousness. I have therefore decided after weighing all the relevant considerations, including the views of the security forces and after consultations with Her Majesty's Government in the United Kingdom last Thursday, to exercise, where necessary, the powers of detention and internment vested in me as Minister of Home Affairs.'

Meanwhile as the arrests went on Faulkner, locked away in solitude in Stormont Castle, signed Order after Order serving detention on those who, he had been assured, were the cause of all his security trouble.

Each order read:

CIVIL AUTHORITIES (SPECIAL POWERS) ACTS
NORTHERN IRELAND. 1922–1943.

ORDER FOR DETENTION OF SUSPECTED PERSONS.

To: The Officer in Charge of the place of detention in the 'Maidstone'.

I, the Right Honourable Brian Faulkner, Minister of Home Affairs for Northern Ireland, by virtue of the powers vested in me by the Civil Authorities (Special Powers) Acts (Northern Ireland) 1922–1943 do hereby order and require you to receive _____, who has been arrested under the provision of the said Civil

Authorities (Special Powers) Acts as a person who is suspected of acting, or having acted, or being about to act in a manner prejudicial to the preservation of the peace or the maintenance of order, at the place of detention in the 'Maidstone' and therein to detain him until he has been discharged by direction of the Attorney General or brought before a Magistrates Court.

Dated this __ day of _____
Minister of Home Affairs for
Northern Ireland Civil Authority.

But within hours of signing hundreds of these documents it had become obvious that all was not going according to plan. Many of those arrested were 'yesterday's men'—veterans from old records or newcomers whose names were well known from student or other protest movements. Some important IRA leaders were taken, but most had got away in good time. It was also clear that the IRA class of 1971 was composed of a new generation quite unknown to those on whom Faulkner had relied on for advice.

For a while the Ministry of Home Affairs and the army claimed great things for the new initiative, but it soon became apparent that, far from causing violence to diminish, internment had released a new flood of communal tension. As the first arrests began, street battles were taking place throughout the Province. Barricades were built and hundreds of homes were set alight as a 'scorched earth' policy gripped the 'peace line' areas. The Farringdon Gardens burnings were flashed from every television station in the world; it was just one incident in a terrible communal migration which created 8,000 refugees in one week in Belfast and eventually uprooted 60,000 people, as each side, fearing the other, sought refuge in an area controlled by fellow Protestants or Catholics.

Internment may not have created these problems, but it added greatly to them and struck a mighty blow at the community organisations dedicated to a policy and programme of reconciliation.

Predictably, the Roman Catholic community erupted with unbelief and anger when internment was announced. Faulkner tried hard to reassure them: 'I want to say a word to my Catholic fellow countrymen. I do not for one moment confuse your community with the IRA or imagine that these acts of terror have been committed in your name or with your approval. I have always had great respect for the God-fearing people— albeit with personal views different from my own—I have met in every part of Ulster. I respect the way in which your religious leaders and many of your public representatives have out-spokenly condemned violence as immoral.

'We are now trying to remove the shadow of fear which hangs over too many of you. I appeal to you to come out and join us in building this community up again—not to restore it simply to what it was, for many of us in the past have failed each other, but to build it on better, sounder and stronger lines. Unless you take the place in the community which awaits you all of us will be the losers. My door is open to any of your leaders, political or religious, who want to discuss how we can now move forward.' [43]

This 'open door' appeal was, no doubt, sincerely meant, for clearly the Prime Minister was convinced that he could make a distinction between security methods and general policy. He was soon to learn how false such a distinction must be: the Roman Catholic community was completely alienated and they responded with a show of solidarity that shook Ulster to its foundations. On 9 August 1971 the Ulster crisis entered a critical phase as Roman Catholics welded together and began to formulate united demands which took on a new and more far-reaching dimension.

Faulkner was soon made aware of Catholic reaction—often from those who a few months earlier had been giving him warm support. The Belfast *Irish News* was brutally frank on the day following internment: 'To ask as he did yesterday for the co-operation of the Catholic community in political affairs, after issuing orders for the arrest and internment of his political opponents is insincerity of the rankest sort. It is the hypocrisy of Tartuffe. Yesterday was a day of awful tragedy.'

For Faulkner it was a very personal tragedy. His apprentice-ship years in government had made him suspect by his Catholic fellow politicians and he had worked hard to create a new image in recent years. His work in Commerce and his early months as Prime Minister had won him a good deal of respect and support among Catholics. August 1971 changed all that. Catholic leaders, North and South, flailed him as few had been flailed before. There were calls on all sides for his removal from office and Mr Lynch on behalf of the Dublin Government demanded the abolition of Stormont. The Catholic Church added its criticism, with Cardinal Conway declaring that 'internment without trial is a terrible power to give a political authority'. The Cardinal also stated his 'abhorrence of internment without trial' and was particularly concerned about its 'one-sided application'.[44]

Even the Pope broke a two-year silence on the Northern Ireland problem with an appeal for peace which included an implied criticism of security policy.

Others more remote from Rome added their criticism. Dr Paisley accused the Prime Minister of introducing internment not as a weapon for constitutional defence, 'but as a weapon of purely political expediency to bolster up his own tottering Premiership'. He was joined in this comment by leading Protestant theoritician Mr Desmond Boal, MP, who made the telling suggestion that the government could have prevented the deterioration of law and order and the disintegration of normal life in the community without 'introducing a legal monstrosity which is not only ineffective but which also can work hardship and injustice and in a sense is as unattractive as the situation it is meant to remedy'.[45]

Faulkner could, of course, point to support for his policy from many quarters, though as time went on it became more muted. Local Protestant Church leaders made a joint statement of general support, balanced with the hope that the system would operate as humanely as possible. The leaders 'recognised the necessity for the introduction of internment' because of 'the continuing violence and bloodshed for which there can be no justification'.[46]

From British politicians, too, there was cautious support, usually in terms regretting the measure and hoping that it would be terminated as soon as possible. The Press were equally

Winner of Pony Championship, Balmoral Show, 1929.

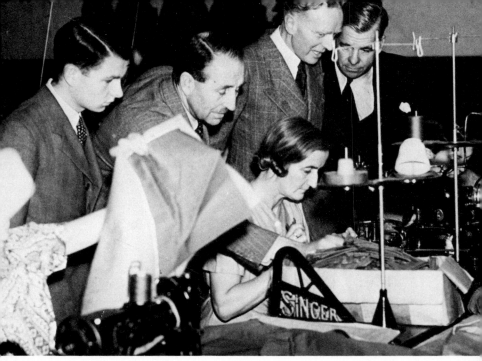

Wartime visit at Belfast Collar Company with Sir Basil Brooke, 1942.

At Downpatrick Races with William Douglas, James Faulkner, and Dr Rodgers MP, 1949.

Wedding day, 10th February, 1951.[4]

With Lord Brookborough and William Douglas, 1958.[5]

At Ulster Unionist Council with R. A. Butler, 1962.[3]

District Commissioner at Pony Club Camp, 1964.[6] .

Parading the Hounds at Balmoral Show, 1966.

Marching with the Orangemen on the 12th July,
Ballynahinch, 1968.[4]

Inspecting new building deck at Harland & Wolff, 1968.[9]

At completion of first house in Glen Road, Andersonstown, crash housing programme for Northern Ireland Housing Trust, 1970.[1]

When both Brian Faulkner and Edward Heath were
Government Chief Whips, 1959.

They meet again as Prime Ministers, 1971.[10]

At Stormont Press Conference after being elected Prime Minister, March, 1971.[4]

Brian Faulkner with his family, Clare, Michael, David and
wife Lucy at their home in Co. Down, 1971.[4]

Leaving Magherahamlet Presbyterian Church after service, 1971.[4]

At 10 Downing Street with William Craig and
the former Prime Minister, Lord O'Neill, 1966.[10]

At Chequers in 1971 with Jack Lynch and Edward Heath.

Speaking from the balcony at Anti-Direct Rule rally, Stormont, 1972.[4]

At Hillsborough with William Whitelaw, April, 1972.[2]

Electioneering.

Speaking at the Grocers Institute Dinner in London, 1973.

Partnership—the end or a new beginning? May 1974. [9]

Members of the former Faulkner Cabinet (*left to right*): Harry West,
Nat Minford, William Long, Robin Baille, John Andrews, John Brooke,
Brian Faulkner, Roy Bradford, Herbert Kirk, William Fitzsimmons,
David Bleakley, March 1971.[8]

Members of the first official meeting of the Executive
(*left to right*): Paddy Devlin, Oliver Napier, Brian Faulkner, John Hume,
Basil McIvor (P. A. Sythes and Ken Bloomfield—secretaries),
John Baxter, Auston Currie, Herbert Kirk, Gerry Fitt, Roy Bradford,
Leslie Morrell, 1st January 1974.[7]

cautious but, except for the Irish papers, basically sympathetic. The liberal *Belfast Telegraph* complained that political as well as security considerations were behind the move but, 'in the state of the country today, Mr Faulkner and his security chiefs had little alternative other than give it a trial'. For the *Daily Mail* the decision meant that the army would no longer have to fight 'with both hands tied behind their backs'. From *The Times* came the comment: 'The situation is one which justifies the use of emergency powers.'

But what the outside world thought of internment was of less importance than its effect on the local situation. Very soon the Northern Ireland Government was faced with a whole series of new problems consequent on the new security policy for which increasingly they had no answer.

The chief Catholic counter attack was organised by the elected representatives of the Social Democratic and Labour Party, the Nationalist Party and the Republican Labour Party. These groups organised a Province-wide and world-supported campaign of civil disobedience in which Stormont suffered the fury and fate felt by Captain Boycott in a previous century of Irish protest.

The conference of representatives expressed 'total opposition to internment' which they regarded as further proof of 'the total failure of the system of Government in Northern Ireland'. A five-point plan was agreed:

1 'We call upon all those who hold public positions in Northern Ireland, whether elected or appointed, to express their opposition to internment by an immediate withdrawal from their positions and to announce it publicly without delay to give evidence that the system of Government set up by the 1920 act has failed.

2 'We call on the general public to participate in this protest by immediately withholding all rents and rates. We expect 100 per cent support from all opponents of internment and all opponents of the Unionist regime.

3 'We will give our full support to all organisations who call meetings to oppose internment and appeal for complete unity in every area.

8

4 'We demand that the military resume the task for which they were sent here—the protection of people and areas against sectarian attack on their homes, pending a political solution.
5 'We call on the Westminster Government to suspend immediately the system of Government in Northern Ireland in view of its absolute failure to provide peace and stability in Northern Ireland and to institute immediate talks on new political and constitutional arrangements.'

The meeting also arranged to send representatives to Westminster and Dublin to express their views. So the Catholic community was welded together in community reaction which could only lead to confrontation.

A few on either side saw the danger of a final community split and tried desperately to keep lines of communication open between Catholic and Protestant communities. They saw that certain forms of civil disobedience were very difficult to reverse and they also feared that rent and rate strikes by one community could just as easily be practised by another.

Typical of a few spokesmen from the Catholic community who warned against the dangers inherent in such a civil disobedience campaign was the comment of Dr G. B. Newe, secretary of the Northern Ireland Council of Social Service: 'Withdrawal from community structures means that true dialogue becomes impossible. One cannot have dialogue with an absent man! And where honest dialogue is inhibited or impossible, a breeding ground for suspicion and mistrust is created.

'Bombing turns people off; so does a rhetoric of exclusion.

'We desperately need a great dose of social charity without which it will be impossible to achieve social justice.' [47]

Faulkner responded to the civil disobedience threat by ordering every department to indicate the extent to which civil disobedience would affect its operations. At once it became clear that there was no agreed response open to the government. The civil service had no guide lines on which to operate. It was also impossible to treat civil disobedience with a cessation of services used in normal circumstances. A whole population could not be cut off from essential supplies. Equally. entire estates could not be evicted for rent arrears; nor could electricity supplies be terminated when there were those who would immediately reconnect.

The Northern Ireland Government soon discovered how much civilisation depends on the consent and co-operation of those who comprise society. Consent had been withdrawn from the system; it would only be restored when security policies (and as time went on, much else) were reversed. Internment had indeed become a Pandora's box.

Faulkner had now reached his ultimate confrontation; and his advice to his colleagues was to 'just grit our teeth and try to pursue a commonsense line which will have both security and political aspects'. Cabinet meetings became increasingly solemn.

When the Northern Ireland Parliament resumed in October after the summer recess Faulkner was still putting a brave face on things and in a defiant speech made a vigorous appeal which was Churchillian in its tone. Speaking to those 'who are working to destroy Ulster', he had this to say: 'We shall resist you. We shall resist you as a Parliament; we shall resist you as a people. To protect our way of life we will make any sacrifice and endure any hardship. We have had divisions which have given comfort to our enemies; we can, and I believe we must, put such divisions behind us. You have destroyed our property, bullied our people and made many live in fear. All of these things only increase our resolve to resist you. You cannot win for we shall not permit it.'

These were strong and eloquent sentiments and they were sincerely offered, but there was a blinding sense of unreality about them. There was now no 'Parliament' of Northern Ireland—there were two (Stormont and an Assembly of the Northern Ireland People); nor was there a 'people'—tragically there were Catholics and Protestants. Internment, aimed at hindering the men of violence, had become the cause of even greater suffering to the whole community.

The essential divide was brought out in an exchange of letters between Faulkner and his Minister of Community Relations, following the latter's resignation in September 1971. In his letter the Minister stated his objection to internment in sentiments which reflected the concern of supporters of the Labour movement and a wider spectrum of public opinion as well: 'I cannot accept that the policy of internment is assisting the cause of law and order. On the contrary I believe that internment is wrong; that this aspect of our policy is a tragic mistake which has made matters worse; further I believe that the terrorists welcome internment for it gives the IRA and other militant groups a sympathy and a hearing on a world-wide scale which otherwise they could not get. In addition the internment controversy handicaps those who are presenting the Northern Ireland case against the campaign of violence.'

The letter also dealt with the community divisive elements of internment—an aspect which cut right across the united Ulster theme which in his June speech Faulkner had been highlighting with signal success.

'Internment is not, as some see it, an isolated security issue; it is a test of policy direction. More than any single issue, it separates Protestant and Roman Catholic and tragically it has alienated the Roman Catholic community at the very moment when community co-operation is most vital.'

Again the letter stresses the United Ulster point: 'In fact, in the Ulster of today we just cannot have internment and a united community. And without a united community a really worthwhile Province is impossible. Those who think otherwise betray a dangerous degree of political insensitivity.'

Faulkner's response to the points made was muted and thoughtful, but unrepentant: 'It is not internment which has divided the community, but continuing violence. The ultimate responsibility for the decision on internment was, of course, mine as Minister of Home Affairs and I took it only when I could see no other way to clear a murderous organisation off the streets and will be more than happy to reverse it when it is clear that by that act I am not simply letting terrorists off the leash again.' [48]

For a further six months Faulkner carried on trying desperately to combine security and political initiatives. But increasingly as he became absorbed in the security problems his wider political plans became impossible or (as with his enlightened Mater Hospital decision and parliamentary reforms) went unnoticed in the growing waves of violence and the public reaction to that violence.

By New Year 1972 few believed that Faulkner had long to go. However, he had no intention of resigning and knew that he had no serious rival in Stormont. What he did not realise was that Edward Heath had no intention of allowing anyone to replace him. He was preparing more far-reaching plans of his own: Direct Rule from Westminster. Already in the closing months of 1971 many hints were given by Whitehall that a fundamental reassessment was being considered. Cabinet Ministers in Belfast were aware that both Heath and Maudling were toying with some very new and radical ideas for government in the Province. Only Brian Faulkner seemed unaware that plans for a take-over were well advanced.

Matters came to a climax early in 1972. It was clear that the security operation was not going well and military sources were pressing hard for a complete transfer of security powers to London. These demands became even more pressing after the shooting in Londonderry by the army of thirteen civilians during a demonstration in January. These tragic killings, which passed into history as 'Bloody Sunday', made a dramatic impression on London thinking and probably more than any other single incident sealed the Direct Rule decision. When the end came it came suddenly. Faulkner was invited to meet Heath and his colleagues in Downing Street. There, at a meeting on 22 March 1972, the Prime Minister put it to him bluntly: the United Kingdom Government had decided to take over complete control of security matters, including all matters to do with the courts in Northern Ireland; the Stormont Government could continue in office, but with much reduced local powers.

For Brian Faulkner this was an offer of 'semi-colonial' status and he gave the prompt rejection which, no doubt, Heath was expecting. Under Section 75 of the Government of Ireland Act there could be no argument—London was supreme and William Whitelaw was dispatched to take over Faulkner's crumbling empire.

For Stormont it was the end and for Faulkner, too, it looked like final defeat. But by an ironical twist of fate Heath's intervention, more than anything else, gave Faulkner an opportunity to survive and to revive his fortunes. No longer was he bedevilled by internment and the other security problems which had diverted him from more positive programmes. From now on the odium and difficulty of security matters passed to the British Government and the address for future complaints would be the Westminster Secretary of State for Northern Ireland. Henceforth, Ulster politicians were required to think within a new framework of political attitudes. Everyone was being offered an opportunity to start anew; the old Stormont was gone and a New Ulster was on the agenda.

'Chance favours the mind that is prepared.' Faulkner had been thinking about such plans for a long time. The challenge was now a real one: to cast aside the habits and political assumptions of a lifetime.

In March 1972 Brian Faulkner had arrived at the most important cross-roads of his life.

CHAPTER NINE

Moment of Truth

'Direct Rule', as the Westminster take-over of the Stormont administration in March 1972 was called, was a traumatic experience for the people of Northern Ireland. Many were fearful of the development; others saw it as a necessary step in the creation of a new and better Province; but there were few who welcomed the event without reservations.

Most Ulster people, however, recognised the decision of the British Government to rule the Province directly from London as a watershed, ending the political arrangement imposed by the Government of Ireland Act, 1920. Mr Heath's intervention had destroyed the power monopoly enjoyed by the Unionist Party; it was regarded as inevitable that any new framework created would have to take into account the religious balance of the population and the tensions associated with the crisis before and since 1969. No doubt the planners in Whitehall had some such plan in mind when they advised the move in March 1972; equally clearly, they were less aware of the difficulties which lay ahead or of the grave new options which would appear as confidence between Belfast and London eroded.

For Brian Faulkner the actual moment of Direct Rule was bitter. He had trusted Edward Heath and had been confident that the trust was reciprocated. The two men had known each other throughout their political careers and shared much in common. They had been Whips together, each had been in Board of Trade departments at the same time, and each had gained the top office in government. Socially they came from similar backgrounds and had fought a lone battle to the summit. Even their personalities were related—both were strong willed, not all that at ease on the gregarious occasion, and enjoyed the more solitary pastime of sailing. But between them there could be no real parity of esteem. Each was, no doubt, determined to have his own way, but in such a confrontation Heath had the advantage: Section 75 of the Government of Ireland Act gave Westminster the final authority in Northern Ireland affairs. Heath was also anxious that nothing should happen in Northern Ireland to interfere with his European policy. Already embarrassing questions had been raised by EEC colleagues, and on security, in particular, the Ulster situation had involved the United Kingdom Government internationally in a difficult defence of the policy—for example, by derogation from the European Human Rights Convention.

Faulkner recognised all these difficulties, but was still confident of the Prime Minister's support. He had been assured by his frequent visits to Downing Street that all was well—indeed, at the height of the newspaper rumours about a Westminster intervention he had been sent a telegram with which to assure his Cabinet colleagues. The telegram which read, 'These articles are pure speculation', raised a great cheer of relief among Faulkner's supporters—only much later was it noted that the message did not deny the allegations made. At this time the basic message conveyed to the Unionist Party was one of 'Trust Heath'; Faulkner believed firmly that he had established a special relationship with the British Premier which would preserve the constitutional *status quo*.

For these reasons Faulkner felt a sense of personal affront when he received Heath's ultimatum on 22 March 1972. He had come to the meeting at Downing Street, along with his Deputy, Senator J. L. O. Andrews, believing that agreed new initiatives would be discussed. As he stated later, he had gone fully prepared to acknowledge that in defeating the violence, military means would have to be buttressed by realistic political proposals, designed to unite the communities and detach them from any sympathy of support for violent men. The Northern Ireland Government had already submitted a comprehensive letter of proposals in preparation for such a discussion. But instead of the expected conference, Faulkner found himself faced, not with a wider-ranging review of all these aspects, or

'with a comprehensive, coherent and final "package" of proposals', but with a proposition which he held to be wholly
unacceptable—that all statutory and executive responsibility
for law and order should be vested in the United Kingdom
Parliament and Government. These included criminal law
and procedure (including the organisation and appointments to
the courts); public order; prisons and penal establishments;
the creation of new penal offences; special powers; the public
prosecuting power; and the police. And, as Faulkner stated
later: 'Even these radical changes were simply to pave the way
for further entirely open-ended discussions with continuing
speculation and uncertainty.'

Altogether it was very advanced political surgery. It was an
operation unacceptable to Faulkner and his Cabinet.

Faulkner did not hesitate. He had already stated on many
previous occasions (and this Heath knew) that his government
would not operate under such conditions which he regarded as
'an acceptance of totally baseless criticism of stewardship'.
He indicated immediately that he was not interested in maintaining a Stormont that would be 'a mere sham, or a face-
saving charade'. His resignation and that of his Cabinet followed, delayed only by the few days requested by Heath to
ensure that there should be no breach in the orderly government of the country until the necessary transfer legislation
passed through Westminster.[49]

On his return to Belfast, Faulkner issued a last message as
Prime Minister to the people of Northern Ireland. He was sad
and serious, but unrepentant. After outlining the events leading
up to the final decision, he warned the British Government that
many people would draw 'a sinister and depressing message
from these events—that violence can pay; that violence does
pay; that those who shout, lie, denigrate and even destroy
can earn for themselves an attention that responsible conduct
and honourable behaviour do not'. He was also angry, but his
anger was controlled. He warned about the danger of making
matters worse through irresponsible reaction: 'I ask our people
at this difficult and trying time to remain calm and on no
account to be led by unwise agitation into possible confrontation

with the security forces, which have been making such tremendous sacrifices on our behalf.' Then his final pledge: 'We will
work, with total determination and utter firmness, but responsibly and under the law, to ensure that the voice of the Ulster
majority—which is not a sectarian majority but a majority of
responsible people loyal to the Crown—is heard loud and clear
throughout the land.' [50]

Faulkner's initial anger was considerable and for a while he
retaliated by lunging out at Heath at political meetings in
Northern Ireland and Britain (and later in the USA). He
rarely indulges in a counter-attack which is personal, but when
he decides to do so he can be biting in retort. He made many
comparisons with various forms of dictatorship and he accused
Heath of betraying the Province and of trying to set up a
'coconut colony'; he also warned that the British Government
were releasing forces which they did not understand and might
not be able to control. Such sentiments made a considerable
impression on the Ulster public and began to win back some
of the support which had been lost in the period following
internment. (When some months later the *Belfast Telegraph*
carried out a leadership support poll, 44 per cent of the
Protestant vote went to Faulkner, with Craig and Paisley
getting 15 per cent and 13 per cent respectively.) Heath, too,
noted these attacks and from then on relationships between the
two leaders cooled rapidly; when they met later at the Sunningdale Conference it was obvious to the other participants
that the 'special relationship' had become one of wary coolness.
Some regarded it as distinctly icy. As one observer later recalled:
'Heath was determined to drive Faulkner into the ground.' [51]

Faulkner's attitude to local 'collaborators' was equally icy.
To the suggestion that an Advisory Commission should be set
up to assist William Whitelaw's Northern Ireland Department,
he was completely unhelpful, only wondering, in an indelicate
and brutal phrase, which people would 'crawl out' to serve
this 'undemocratic imposition'. Such sentiments coming from
such a quarter made it very difficult for the Commission to
start. Many prominent people became reluctant to serve and
those who did so were subject to considerable initial abuse.

Faulkner later seemed to regret these statements and, though he did not co-operate with the Commission, he left it to get on with its difficult task. Other immediate threats were equally disturbing to Whitehall. Most worrying was his warning: 'God forbid that we should ever have to exercise our powerful veto by paralysing an unacceptable system of government imposed on us.'

Faulkner, of course, was not alone in regretting the passing of Stormont. He got the support of constituency organisations throughout the country and even the Vanguard leader, William Craig, felt able to say: 'Our Prime Minister did his best and he was shabbily treated.' More surprising, influential voices in the Roman Catholic community expressed regrets. From G. B. Newe, his Catholic colleague in the Cabinet, came a comment which gave expression to the sense of something Irish having been lost: 'As an Irishman I am sorry that an Irish Parliament has been disbanded. Of course, I would have preferred Northern Ireland to be governed by Irishmen rather than by Englishmen. I hope that sooner or later an Irish administration will return to Northern Ireland.'

Eddie McAteer, the leader of the Nationalist Party, was equally conscious of the Irish dimension: 'This is a day of sadness for I find no joy in being ruled from the remote and insensitive smoke-rooms of Westminster. Faced with the choice I would prefer to be ruled by Protestant Irishmen than by Englishmen.' And then, a percipient hint at things to come: 'Perhaps we will now at last find common ground as equal people without sectarian power, perhaps as brothers "agin" the Government. A terrible beauty has not quite been born, but the pregnancy is well advanced.'

One hundred and seventy-two years earlier something of the same sense of loss had been felt in Ireland when the Act of Union closed another Irish Parliament.

Faulkner, never given to longterm forecasts, preferred to get on with the task in hand. As his initial anger passed, he began to look for ways to regain the initiative and to make sure that he retained his grasp on the leadership of the country. The power vacuum was worrying so he decided to fill it as quickly as possible. By leading the local criticism against Westminster he had already managed to behave like a Prime Minister-in-Waiting and with his assured wealth he had no difficulty in continuing the life-style associated with the office. He also had support behind the scenes from top civil servants who, though they were local to the incoming administration, felt deep down that one day their former ministers would return.

But Faulkner also realised the realities of Westminster power and the need to re-establish himself at home and abroad. In a spectacular tour of England and Scotland (followed later by a coast-to-coast visit to America) he began his national and international comeback, presenting his case as 'a loyal subject who had done his best' and who had been sacrificed by the appeasement policy of a British Prime Minister who had 'a very poor opinion indeed of the British public's moral fibre'. This was popular material among the Tory rank-and-file and very rapidly regained him a firm following in the Conservative Party. Even the Bow Group were impressed and provided an influential London platform at the Royal Commonwealth Society rooms at which he spelt out the ways in which he regarded Heath's initiative as 'morally and politically wrong'. He very astutely developed the theme that London intellectuals had taken over from the down-to-earth politicians in Belfast (though, some of his listeners must have murmured, 'Indeed, they have and near time, too'!): 'For Mr Heath and Mr Wilson and Mr Thorpe the affairs of Northern Ireland are a matter of political science . . . for us in Ulster it is a matter of life and death.' The Tory Party was increasingly impressed by this point of view and a few months later, when Faulkner addressed the Conservative annual conference, he was given a rapturous welcome—neither Edward Heath nor William Whitelaw seemed to enjoy the occasion but, no doubt, they took the point.

While re-establishing his support in Britain, Faulkner at the same time turned to the problem of reorganising his Unionist home base. Since 1969 dangerous schisms had appeared and he felt the need to build a united front. Two men, in particular, were challenging the former monolithic unity of the Unionist

Party—the Right Hon. William Craig and the Rev. Dr Ian R. K. Paisley. Each man already represented a considerable following, but Direct Rule was giving their views a new relevance, which could not be ignored and which had to be challenged by a dynamic alternative. Craig and Paisley had much in common, but in reality they could never be more than uneasy partners; their policies set them apart and so too did their personalities.

Craig, one of Ulster's most enigmatic figures, was for many years the protegé and mainstay of Terence O'Neill. He entered the Stormont Parliament in 1960 and, gaining fast promotion, he remained a powerful member of the Cabinet until his dismissal in 1969. By that time his verbal indiscretions and intellectual excursions into various forms of dominion status and local independence had begun to alarm the Prime Minister more than the prospect of having to do without his valued assistance.

Since removal from office this solitary and somewhat grave figure has emerged as one of Ireland's most controversial political personalities. A strange mixture of zealot and visionary, he has won an international reputation for utterances which have a distinctly chilling effect on many of his listeners, particularly if they happen to be Roman Catholics.

Craig is also gently spoken and immaculately polite. His professional critics may make the quip that he would have made an excellent hanging judge. Perhaps he would—but they may rest assured that with great and never failing courtesy he could have made a capital sentence sound like an invitation to a wedding. One can almost hear the condemned man saying: 'Thank you very much, your Honour.'

But behind this mildness, there is a determination of steel.

Ian Paisley, Faulkner's other great rival in 1971, is equally determined, but there the comparison with William Craig ends. One has to look for Craig in a room—Ian Paisley's presence can never be overlooked. By 1971, with only one year in Parliament, the Member for North Antrim had become something of an Irish legend; even in the Belfast shipyard, Europe's biggest crane 'Goliath' is known to the locals as 'Big Ian'. The story of the leader of the Free Presbyterian Church in Ireland is very much that of the local boy made good. No silver spoon here—it is a tale of personal achievement, based on hard work, supported by a keen native intelligence and a harsh but compelling turn of phrase, full of earthy wit. Even ardent Roman Catholics have been known to smile at some of his more outlandish descriptions of His Holiness: 'Old Red Socks' or 'The slanderous bachelor who lives on the banks of the Tiber'.

He is in many ways very much the ebullient Irish country parson, expansive in body and spirit, and at peace, if rather rumbustiously, with God and his neighbour—but, of course, no friend of the local landed gentry whose snubs he has never forgiven.

But Ian Paisley is no figure of fun—he is a complicated mixture of the social radical and the political reactionary. Cross him in argument and a man of wrath takes over. The transformation is remarkable. All who stand in the way must go (and many there have been). In such encounters a giant's strength appears and it is used like a giant; the man becomes a vehicle for crusades with an elemental fury behind them.

Craig and Paisley together are associated with a message which is essentially tribal at heart. Individually their relations with men of all faiths may be excellent, but their philosophy and language is totally ill-suited to the pluralistic society of Northern Ireland. Modern Ulster needs policies which lead to Protestant and Roman Catholic reconciliation; William Craig and Ian Paisley offer no such programme.

Faulkner's efforts to accommodate his two great rivals for Unionist support had never been substantial and even in the crisis of 1972 he did not go out of his way to placate either. With Craig he went further than with Paisley and appeared at the great public rally of some 200,000 who turned up before Stormont on its last day's sitting in March to mark their support for the local Parliament and to show their defiance of the new rulers. It was an impressive if sabre-rattling occasion and politicians representing many shades of Unionism attended. Faulkner used the day to make certain that he got parity of appearance with Craig and other Unionist leaders, so making certain that in the last moments of Stormont he remained a central character.

But though an uneasy public reconciliation was indicated at this meeting the rapprochement did not go deep; each had made a completely different analysis of the situation which led them in opposing policy directions. Faulkner was fundamentally repelled by both the theory and practice of the Vanguard movement led by his old colleague. For example, the call for a political strike, closing down all essential services and effectively severing all means of communication inside the Province and between Northern Ireland and Britain had been a frightening affair. Severe damage had also been done to life and property. Faulkner was appalled by such tactics; they offended against his sense of citizenship obligation and were at variance with his lifelong habit of separating politics and business. He condemned the strikes as 'economic madness' and asked that there should be no further disruption of industry or the economic life of the Province. At the same time, sensing the danger to the economy, he began to draw a distinction between the political duties of William Whitelaw and the social and economic responsibilities of the office. He promised to meet the Secretary of State (an offer very rapidly accepted) to talk about proposals 'to meet the needs of the people in terms of jobs, homes and hope for the future'. Already, after only a week out of office, he had begun to make sure that he had a say at the centre of things.

But even more than the immediate tactics of the Vanguard Movement, it was their long-term aim which worried Faulkner most. For some time Craig had been talking about a fundamentally new relationship between Ulster and Britain, in which Ulster would achieve, ideally by negotiation, an independent status with appropriate links with the Crown and the Commonwealth. In view of the impossibility of getting local and national consent for such an aim many people regarded such a policy as, in essence, a UDI demand. Faulkner believed that programmes based on a thesis of independence were 'absolute rubbish'; there was therefore an unbridgeable gulf between him and the Vanguard leader. The nature of the divide became apparent during 1972 as Faulkner and Craig each made their proposals. For Faulkner the challenge was one of working within the options offered by Direct Rule and the constitutional guarantees offered by Westminster, while at the same time working towards the re-establishment of a local parliament. Vanguard, for its part, looked for a fresh Constitution which would allow for 'a new model of political relationships in the British Isles in which Great Britain, Ulster and Eire would be independent entities with, hopefully, better relationships between them'. Also at another Vanguard rally it was resolved to work for the restoration of the Northern Ireland Parliament 'preferably within the United Kingdom, but if necessary without'.

It was the suggestion of a Northern Ireland Parliament 'without' the United Kingdom that caused Faulkner to swerve most swiftly from the Vanguard organisation and which undoubtedly convinced him that no accommodation could be made with its supporters. For some months he persevered with Craig, trying to involve him in joint Unionist approaches to the British Government, but increasingly he felt it impossible to establish points of contact. Very soon he was hurling the 'UDI' accusation directly at the Movement—no reconciliation was possible.

Equal difficulties lay in the way of an agreement with Ian Paisley. The Democratic Unionist Party leader was quite clear in his denunciation of UDI and had prepared a very different response to Direct Rule—total integration with Britain. This demand was described by Craig as a 'gimmick' and, except for Enoch Powell, it found little favour among political leaders in Britain or Ireland. Emotionally, however, it had greater appeal than UDI and even Faulkner in his speech to the Bow Group saw merit in it. If something better than a 'sham Stormont' were not available then he would settle for nothing less than a full alignment with the rest of the United Kingdom 'on the Scottish pattern, giving adequate representation at Westminster, full British standards and a total equality with fellow citizens in Great Britain'.[52]

However, always a realist, Faulkner soon saw in subsequent

meetings with British Ministers that integration was impossible. He also recognised that to press for such a policy as the only acceptable Ulster safeguard was to draw Belfast and London into a constitutionally dangerous argument. In these circumstances, he believed that the best way to safeguard the Province as an integral part of the United Kingdom was through the re-establishment of an effective local Parliament. For these reasons he believed that talk about total integration was counter productive and diverted Ulster people away from the essential task which was to ensure that the new constitutional settlement which must come was in the best interests of Northern Ireland. So, as with William Craig, so with Ian Paisley no accommodation was possible. Equally each of these gentlemen was in no mood to be accommodating to the former Prime Minister.

Faulkner's attempts in the early weeks of Direct Rule to probe the varied ranks of Unionism disturbed many local observers and many accused him of prevarication. The Alliance Party, for instance, were critical of the association with Craig: 'The unholy wedlock between Mr Faulkner and Mr Craig was nothing more than the real Faulkner, the old Faulkner, the Faulkner of the Longstone Road, re-emerging now that he has nothing to lose.' In similar vein, John Hume, SDLP spokesman, saw it as: 'Just the case of Faulkner reverting to type.' But there were also those who saw evidence that he was feeling out the ground around him and testing opinion among the 'grass-roots'; and his speeches on such mass meeting occasions also ensured that mainstream Unionist opinion was heard. In any case, having made his reconnoitre, in typical fashion he decided to retire to reassess the situation.

Around this time, Brian Walker (Director of OXFAM, but then leader of the New Ulster Movement), advised the local political leaders to lower their voices. In particular, he advised Faulkner to take a very long holiday and 'reassess the entirely new situation given to both communities by the Westminster initiatives'. It was good advice and Faulkner took it. In April 1972, after the most intense political period of his life, he set-off along with his wife on a lengthy tour of France, Switzerland and Italy. It was a restful and reflective time (though on one occasion he was seen wandering in the Memorial Gardens in Geneva regarding the famous Martyrs—and no doubt wondering what was in store for him!) during which he made a fundamental reassessment which was to alter radically his own future and that of the community he aspired to lead; he began to realise with compelling clarity that a new Ulster could only be assembled within the framework of a new dynamic. And the dynamic was—partnership.

When Faulkner returned to Belfast his mind was made up: a new accommodation must be sought with Westminster within the context of the United Kingdom and in accordance with the concept of 'an active, permanent and guaranteed role' for both communities in Northern Ireland.

Ideas like these meant setting aside the political habits of a lifetime. Also revolutionary, for a Unionist leader, was acceptance of the notion that consent was a new imperative for all in Ulster. And real consent demanded a two-way process, Protestant *and* Catholic. The unthinkable had at last become thinkable. There was only one way forward: Protestants and Catholics together in a shared community government.

CHAPTER TEN

Ulster Rubicon

Faulkner's decision in the summer of 1972 to move towards a politics of partnership could not have been easy. He belonged to a party which, along with the traditional nationalists, had accepted the sectarian divide as a by-product of history about which little could be done. The settlement given by the Government of Ireland Act, 1920, had been an uneasy one. The Act itself pleased few. For Unionists it was an unhappy compromise, weakening integration with the rest of the United Kingdom, and for Nationalists it represented a defeat, symbolised by the border and the Stormont Parliament. As a result, in the formative years of the state the established political groupings kept one another at arms' length, each in their own Protestant or Catholic ghetto. Community structures tended to follow the community divide, and such an alignment made it impossible to achieve a sharing of power across the sectarian divide or to enjoy the changes of government normally associated with western democracy.

The crisis of 1969 brought into question the whole system of government in Northern Ireland and by 1972 the British Government had begun to delineate a power pattern for the future, based on the stipulation that the future government of the Province must 'no longer be based upon any single party if that party draws its support and its elected representatives virtually entirely from only one section of a divided community'.[53]

It was inside this situation that the politicians in Northern Ireland in the post Direct Rule period were required to operate—a 'new politics' was being demanded by Westminster. Neither Unionists nor Nationalists took easily to the change. Fifty years of Stormont politics was not easily put aside—nor was it easy to adopt political practices which even in Britain (Proportional Representation and National Governments, for example) were the subject of controversy.

Faulkner, though anxious to move away from the pre-1969 patterns, shared some of the doubts about untried constitutional innovations. As recently as 3 November 1971, he had outlined to the Commons his detailed opposition to what he described as 'P.R. Government'. He was certainly anxious to create a situation 'where a self-respecting man, with the support of the people he represents, would feel that he does good' by coming to Stormont. But this meant for him the development of a committee system which would involve the opposition in a policy-scrutiny operation; it did not mean 'the idea that, as of right, opposition members should be guaranteed a proportion of Cabinet positions, provided for in new constitutional arrangements'. He did not believe that a Cabinet formed directly proportionate to the strength of the various parties in Parliament was a practical proposition: 'I must say quite bluntly that in my view it could not conceivably work and certainly I for one would never wish to serve in such a Cabinet.'

He was particularly concerned about the difficulties of maintaining Cabinet unity. He felt that if the combative elements of Ulster politics were fused it was likely to produce a 'Bedlam Cabinet', a kind of fragmentation bomb virtually certain to fly apart at the first meeting: 'It would be like a British Cabinet based on the combined talents of Michael Foot and Gerald Nabarro, Enoch Powell and James Callaghan, Harold Wilson and Edward Heath.' He ruled out as 'wholly impracticable and unrealistic this kind of constitutional change in the Cabinet system'.

Two years and two months after this speech was made Brian Faulkner was presiding as Chief Minister over a Cabinet even more diverse than his British 'Bedlam'—a measure of how dangerous it is to use the word 'never' in politics!

But, politically speaking, November 1971 and the summer of 1972 belonged to different epochs. Direct Rule had created a new situation in which much that had happened in the past was no longer applicable; instead, new options were being provided.

Faulkner was well aware of these changes and realistic enough to recognise the need to work within them. During the summer he had also had an opportunity to have lengthy discussions with Whitelaw and other ministers. He began to realise that, though they would not be deflected from the principles they had formulated, they were willing and anxious to co-operate with those Ulster politicians who represented an effective area of political opinion.

The influence of William Whitelaw at this time was considerable. He was something new in Irish politics—an Englishman whom everyone trusted. Even when deemed wrong he was forgiven with a friendly, 'He means well, anyway', comment. This avuncular and shrewd Tory giant was the right man in the right place at the right time. In a land of superlative talkers he talked everyone into a kind of sanity and made possible combinations which not many politicians in Ireland or elsewhere had previously attempted. Few English statesmen have left such a decisive mark on Ireland in such a short time; when he left in 1973 there was great regret and apprehension at his departure.

Following the introduction of Direct Rule, Whitelaw was involved in intensive discussions with all shades of opinion in Northern Ireland. Faulkner had taken part in these talks and between him and the Secretary of State a greatly improved relationship developed which restored some of the confidence shattered by the events of March. Similar talks with other political leaders established points of agreement between several major political groupings, and when inter-party talks were held at Darlington in September it was obvious that signs of a political thaw were appearing. The delegates of the Northern Ireland Labour Party, in particular, long active as advocates of community government, took the opportunity to press their partnership views anew. Other groups had also begun to move in the same direction. Faulkner was part of this changing process and though in large measure he submitted proposals which fell far short of a community government concept, he did show evidence of growing closer to the views of his opponents.

In particular, from the publication of the Green Paper

(October 1972) which followed the Darlington conference, there was growing evidence that Faulkner and the Social Democratic and Labour Party were beginning to close some of the gaps between them. He agreed with them, for instance, that there should be some structural changes at Stormont and in the membership of the Parliament. On the question of a voting system there was some common ground. PR was suggested by most groups; Faulkner, though not keen on the idea, raised no fundamental objections. (PR later became an important instrument for political change in the Province.)

On Faulkner's side the greatest shift in opinion was clearly that concerning the creation of a Council of Ireland. Throughout his career there had always been an 'Irish dimension' to his thinking, which distinguished him from many of his more traditional colleagues. Certainly he was more at ease with his Southern neighbours than many of his public attitudes would seem to indicate; his business and social contacts in the South were many and varied. What surprised the Darlington delegates was the extent to which he was prepared to carry his North-South co-operation. He insisted that the task of securing a stable and lasting settlement in Northern Ireland could be made 'significantly easier' by the co-operation of the government and people of Southern Ireland, and, provided proper guarantees were given on security and constitutional matters, he believed that it would be possible to form a joint 'Irish inter-Governmental Council' with equal membership from the governments of Northern Ireland and the Irish Republic. He envisaged that such a Council should have special functions in the economic and social field. Here, again, he was coming closer to the aspirations of the Roman Catholic community and of the largely Catholic SDLP.

In the memorandum offered by the SDLP came an equally significant change of emphasis. There was the suggestion of an 'entirely new concept' of Irish unity, of one that would have 'the agreement of and consent of all sections of opinion in Ireland' and of machinery that would give 'full confidence to the Protestant community in the North'. This new recognition of the fears and rights of Protestants brought the party appreciably closer to the Unionists and was an important stage towards ultimate agreement that no change should take place in the constitutional status of the North without the consent of a Northern majority. This was an important recognition of a reality which had been ignored for fifty years; it greatly strengthened the possibility of unity between the two Northern communities.

The Darlington Conference gave Faulkner a new confidence. From then, a new mobility is discernible in his policies and, through him, in the official attitudes of his party. He was greatly strengthened in his campaign inside the party by the publication of the British Government's White Paper—Northern Ireland Constitutional Proposals, which appeared in March 1973. These proposals, which had the backing of all sides at Westminster, left no room for doubt among Ulster politicians. There was, indeed, to be a new Ulster and, as promised, a new regional government would be permitted, but only on terms which would bind 'majority and minority' to support the new political arrangement. Nor was there to be any doubt where ultimate sovereignty lay: 'It is the responsibility of the United Kingdom Parliament to determine how Northern Ireland shall be governed as a part of the United Kingdom.' The White Paper also defined a three-fold pattern of obligations with which any settlement must be consistent:

'a)   The United Kingdom as a whole has an obligation to those of its citizens who live in Northern Ireland to afford them the fullest protection of the rule of law; to secure their fundamental rights and freedoms; and to work towards the realisation for them of United Kingdom standards of living, employment and social conditions.

'b)   Those who live in Northern Ireland as part of the United Kingdom have an obligation to respect the decisions of the Crown in Parliament and to play their part in creating and in upholding an equitable political settlement.

'c)   Those who wish to see the achievement of Irish unity, which can only be on a basis of consent, have an obligation to accept that such consent does not at present exist, and—without prejudice to their aspirations—to assist in the achievement on a constitutional basis of peace, equality and prosperity.'

In order to achieve community co-operation consistent with these obligations the Government insisted that the new Executive to be formed in Northern Ireland must not be based upon any single party 'if that party draws its support and its elected representatives virtually from only one section of a divided community'. Power-sharing (Protestant and Catholic politicians working together in government and broadly representative of the community) would become the principle on which devolved government would rest—and the Paper was clear that power would only be transferred from Westminster when this condition was met. The principle of parity of esteem between the two Ulster communities was further strengthened by proposals for a Charter of Human Rights, providing additional restraints against the abuse of legislative and executive powers and special machinery to deal with job discrimination. (Later Lord Feather was appointed to chair the Commission.)

More revolutionary than generally realised at the time was the proposal to elect the Northern Ireland Assembly by PR. This change opened up entirely new options. In particular, it encouraged the emergence of a considerable group of 'centre' politicians and began the break-up of the two-party sectarian voting pattern which had existed under the simple majority rule.

In return for the expected co-operation of the citizens of Northern Ireland, the White Paper offered considerable guarantees. Firm promises were given: Northern Ireland would remain in the United Kingdom so long as a majority wished it so; the troops would stay as long as they were needed; and massive economic aid was promised. Even the 'Irish dimension' got a favourable mention. A Council of Ireland was envisaged, but only with the consent of 'both majority and minority opinion in Northern Ireland'.

In general, the Northern Ireland Constitution Act 1973 (the new Constitution for Northern Ireland) followed the lines of the White Paper, and though there were reservations about its contents most people were willing to try out the new arrangements.

Faulkner had no doubts about what should be done. As a

loyal citizen of the United Kingdom he recognised his obligation 'to respect the decisions of the Crown in Parliament' and
to play a part in creating and in upholding an equitable political
settlement. He won the party over to his views and in June
1973 led his supporters into the first general election for the new
Assembly.

The general election of 1973 was the first test of the 'new
politics' in Northern Ireland and demanded a declaration of
intent from those who stood as candidates. Faulkner's approach
to the settlement was outlined in a policy document *Peace,
Order and Good Government* which became the manifesto of the
Unionist Party. It was an important document and showed
how far he had travelled in his thinking since Direct Rule,
fifteen months earlier. Gone are the reservations about power-
sharing or a 'Bedlam Cabinet': 'Unionist policy for the Assembly
elections is positive, constructive and forward-looking. It is also
realistic and practical. Given the support of the people of
Ulster we will develop and mould the new Assembly into the
kind of Government and Parliament which Northern Ireland
needs.' This was a very confident appeal. It was also the practical politician speaking—first control the levers of power and
then seek the transformation.

Faulkner also knew by June 1973 that developments were
moving in his favour. It was clear that Westminster (both sides
of Parliament) were anxious to rid themselves of the Ulster
problem as soon as possible; it was also clear (a fact increasingly
recognised by the SDLP and the Catholic population) that the
Dublin Government were just as anxious to avoid direct
responsibility for Northern Ireland affairs. This conjunction
of Dublin and London attitudes influenced strongly the North
Irish politicians in the summer of 1973 as they prepared for
their general election. It began to dawn on them that whatever
the outcome of the contest they were on their own as never
before; that though London and Dublin would be glad to assist
from a distance, at the end of the day the solution to the Ulster
crisis would have to be formulated and implemented among
Ulster people themselves. Mr Whitelaw made this point incessantly and when, later, the equally concerned Merlyn Rees

took over on behalf of a Labour Government he too stressed the point.

Faulkner entered the 1973 election knowing that for the first time in its history the Unionist Party would be unlikely to gain an overall majority. He accepted the logic of the situation and advanced a policy for government based on 'a willing partnership of those who agree sufficiently to provide a cohesive direction of policy'. He had effectively rejected the doctrine of one-party rule still pursued by right-wing election opponents, and by persuading the Unionist Party to accept the policy document he had got his mandate for partnership. Further, during the campaign he managed by an astute piece of word manipulation to obtain freedom to negotiate with his lifelong political opponents in the SDLP. In what seemed an assault on Republicans he insisted: 'I want to make it clear that under no circumstances will I share power with any group whose primary aim is a United Ireland.' Few at the time may have noted the insertion of the word 'primary', just as few had noted its inclusion in the Official Unionist Manifesto, but the word was there on both occasions.

This freedom to negotiate with Catholic politicians was a major development. It cleared the way for effective joint political action between Northern Ireland's religious communities for the first time in the history of the state. Faulkner had made his vital gesture—a gesture which he had been preparing since his return from the continent a year earlier. What was now needed was a response from someone of equal stature in the Catholic political community.

Fortunately for Faulkner such a man was available in the person of Gerard Fitt, MP for West Belfast. Gerry Fitt, one of the most amiable and colourful men in Irish politics, was born in Belfast in 1926 and has lived and worked for most of his life in the dockland area of the city. Leader of the nineteen-strong Social Democratic Labour Party in the Northern Ireland Assembly, he had been associated with trade union and labour politics from his boyhood days. He (like Faulkner) had attended meetings held by the local socialist leader, Harry Midgley, but unlike the young Unionist he had become a ready convert.

Fitt later gravitated to the socialist republicanism of James Connolly, but he has always maintained fraternal links with the British trade union and labour movement. In addition, his impressive ex-service record had given him an acceptance among Protestants denied to most Catholic politicians. Fitt had another advantage. Though as Irish and nationalist as any of his colleagues, his Belfast connection has brought him into contact with a political cross-section of the Province, an advantage which those who come from the remoter and rural areas of the North do not have; it has enabled him to bring to Catholic radicalism a deeper appreciation of the totality of Ulster life than any other nationalist leader. He is emphatically an Ulsterman and, as he puts it, has 'more in common with a Belfast Protestant than a Catholic from Cork'.

But above all else, Fitt is a realist. Like Faulkner, by 1972 he had come to terms with the facts of local life and had realised the need to practise survival politics; he has no time for 'long-distance Republicans commenting far from the action'. Fitt's influence was evident in the programme of his party in the Assembly election and was particularly important in moving SDLP members towards accepting the principle of local consent. This local emphasis was far removed from the traditional nationalist stress on 'the whole Irish nation' and made possible a fundamental realignment in Northern politics which contributed substantially to the partnership formula.

At a more personal level, the association between the Unionist and SDLP leaders was made easier by the fact that they had known each other throughout their long political careers. Most of their colleagues were of a recent intake—even in the new Executive a majority originated from as recently as 1969 and several were of 1973 vintage. Down the years the two men had got to know and respect each other's qualities. Fitt, for instance, had often praised Faulkner and had differentiated between the Unionist leader and the party he led: 'I personally believe that Brian Faulkner has shown remarkable courage in trying to drag the Unionist Party into the twentieth century.'

Even the public often thought of them as a pair. Neither were regarded as men who stuck rigidly to points of dogma and each had a popular reputation of being something of a 'fixer'. They were known as men who believed in getting things done, and though they were sometimes accused of dealing an occasional card from the bottom of the political pack, they were widely regarded as people who would keep the game going. Such was the local folk-lore about these two party stalwarts who, in the summer of 1973, began to move towards a union without precedent in Ulster politics.

Oddly enough, when the association was finalised it received rapid and widespread acceptance. A few years earlier such a combination would have seemed impossible; by 1973 there was a touch of inevitability about it. The time for the idea had come.

But more than anything else, the merger between Faulkner and Fitt was a symbolic partnership between two people which made possible the greater partnership between two communities. From that point onwards the unspoken question was increasingly evident throughout Ulster: 'If lifelong opponents like Gerry Fitt and Brian Faulkner get together, why not the rest of us?'

The actual achievement of a community government came swiftly in the autumn of 1973. After the election results, William Whitelaw initiated a series of talks separately and jointly with the leaders of the three main pro-Assembly groups—Unionists, SDLP and Alliance. The unity between these three had been established at the first and turbulent meeting of the Assembly at Stormont on 31 July 1973. On that occasion, after wild scenes which received world-wide publicity, the pro-Assembly groups voted down an attempt to challenge the selection of a Speaker for the new body. It was an acrimonious but important confrontation. When the vote was taken the pro-Assembly members had won by an easy margin, but the implication of the methods used against them served to persuade the three parties to move towards closer co-operation. Weeks of intense discussions followed and eventually on 21 November 1973 William Whitelaw was able to announce to a surprised world and an even more surprised Province that agreement had been reached; an Executive-designate had been formed; a community government, headed by Mr Faulkner, with Mr Fitt as Deputy, was to be established for Northern Ireland.

But before the Executive 'designate' could become an Executive 'appointed', there was one further stage—one which later was to involve Faulkner in conflict with many of his supporters—the Sunningdale Conference convened by the British Government at Sunningdale, Berkshire in December. The British Government had indicated in its White Paper of March 1973 that, following elections to the Assembly, it would invite the government of the Republic of Ireland and the leaders of the elected representatives of Northern Ireland opinion to participate with them in a conference to discuss how the three objectives set out in the Paper for discussion might best be pursued. These objectives were:

'a) the acceptance of the present status of Northern Ireland, and of the possibility—which would have to be compatible with the principle of consent—of subsequent change in that status;

b) effective consultation and co-operation in Ireland for the benefit of North and South alike; and

c) the provision of a firm basis for concerted governmental and community action against terrorist organisations.'

The SDLP members of the Executive-designate were interested, in particular, in the 'Irish dimension' element in the proposed agenda; Unionists were particularly anxious to get effective joint action on security matters; and for all concerned there was a good deal of unspoken agreement that a successful conference was part of the price that had to be paid to enable the new Northern Ireland Executive to operate with success.

Faulkner had no doubts about the decision to go to Sunningdale. He felt that the Province had managed to regain much: a regional government was to be re-established with considerable powers and with growth potential; the border referendum had been decisively pro-Union; and the British Government had given firm guarantees about the future constitutional status of the Province. He was once again to be Chief Minister in Northern Ireland and had become the first leader of that state to speak for a significant proportion of both Protestant and Catholic communities. In addition, he had gained a considerable personal victory at the June general election and his group was still the largest in the Assembly. He could face

Edward Heath with much of his former status; Sunningdale was no trip to Canossa.

Faulkner's task at Sunningdale (December 6, 7, 8 and 9 1973) was made easier by the nature of the opposition that was building up against him at home. The campaign against him was based on an amalgamation similar to that which had brought down O'Neill and which had recently offended the British public by their tactics of obstruction in the new Assembly. Mr Heath's cool attitude to Faulkner also proved a bonus; as pressure from the British Prime Minister increased, so the Northern Ireland delegation drew closer together. Faulkner was also on good terms with Liam Cosgrave. The Southern leader and he had many social contacts in common and, above all, were equally addicted to hunting. They were good companions and got on well together in negotiation.

In the agreed communiqué[54] which was issued at the end of the Conference it was clear that there was merit in Cosgrave's view that there had been 'no winners or no losers'. For the assurance of Northern Unionists came a declaration by the Irish Government that 'there could be no change in the status of Northern Ireland until a majority of the people of Northern Ireland desired a change in that status'. This declaration and one by the British Government supporting 'the wishes of the majority of the people of Northern Ireland' were to be registered at the United Nations. The Conference also agreed that a Council of Ireland would be set up, comprising a Council of Ministers, with a Consultative Assembly having advisory and review functions.

In a more relaxed and trustful situation the agreement made at Sunningdale might have passed into operation without much fuss. But constitutional challenges as to its validity in the Dublin High Court, controversy over the meaning of key clauses, continued IRA violence, and a sweeping victory for anti-Sunningdale candidates in the Westminster general election of March 1974, put a difficult question-mark over the interpretation and implementation of the Agreement.

But whatever the ultimate form of co-operation between Northern Ireland and the Republic, Sunningdale was not a negative occasion. The differences dividing the parties were great. But Liam Cosgrave spoke for many when he said: 'All of us who live today in the island of Ireland have inherited an immensely difficult and complex problem which has brought suffering and death to innocent men and women in each generation. It is a problem which no previous generation in our history—whatever else it may have achieved—was able to resolve. The way is open to us who live in Ireland at this particular time to resolve it.'

Noble sentiments—echoed later by Brian Faulkner.

But for Brian Faulkner and his Province the real and immediate gift was that of partnership. Sunningdale's Irish dimension represented a prospect of things to come on a more leisurely timescale of co-operation; however, community government represented an urgent challenge on which no delay was possible. As an Irish national political journal *Hibernia* noted at the end of 1973: 'The year that is drawing to a close has seen enormous changes in the political scene on this island: a new Executive in the North, tentative agreement on a Council of Ireland, a coalition in the South, and, for both, the first year of membership within the EEC. But the greatest of these developments is that for the first time ever, the representatives of the minority within the Six Counties are to participate in government. For that advance alone, 1973 must be considered a significant year in the history of this still divided island.'

The reality of partnership was given official confirmation on 31 December 1973. Direct Rule ended and Arthur Brian Deane Faulkner was sworn in as Chief Minister of Northern Ireland's first community government.

After twenty-five years of public life Brian Faulkner was starting again in a new political environment. Along with his colleagues he knew the risks and he took his stand: 'We stand here of our own free will in a partnership which seeks to face the realities of life in Northern Ireland today. Can anyone doubt that if this Province is to have good government, we must turn aside from our old divisions. I believe not only that what we are engaged upon is right, but there is no alternative to it.

'I say to the people of Northern Ireland: give this

131

administration the chance to work, as it can, and I believe we can employ more power to do good in Northern Ireland than any of our predecessors.'

From January to May 1974, Faulkner and his inter-party Ministry demonstrated their ability to make Protestant and Roman Catholic partnership a reality. For all concerned, it was a unique but short-lived experience; it deserved a better chance. But the decision of the Sunningdale Conference to associate the great adventure of partnership with a controversial 'Irish dimension' required the new Executive to pioneer too much too quickly. On 15 May a general stoppage in opposition to the Council of Ireland was called by the Ulster Workers' Council and before long the Province was heading for total collapse. The final blow came with the UWC demand that the army should assume responsibility for all services. It was a chilling request; the lurch into the unknown feared by the civil authorities had begun.

At this point, Faulkner, sensing the magnitude of the crisis, announced that he was not prepared for any political reason to see the country destroyed. He resigned on 28 May, giving both sides an opportunity to retreat with honour. The response was dramatic—by next day the strike had ended.[55]

For many, it also seemed the end of the Executive and all it represented. But Faulkner recognised no such implication. For him, resignation had been a personal gesture, used to save the country from certain catastrophe. Looking beyond the immediate crisis his call remained clear. Partnership had become the great imperative; the Province could only remain in the United Kingdom 'on the basis of co-operation between Protestants and Roman Catholics'. It was an urgent appeal to combine Ulster unity with British union. Separatists of all shades were being rejected.

This most pragmatic of Irish politicians had set aside the partisan attitudes of a lifetime in favour of a community stance. It was one in which his own future was at risk; it was one which involved the fate of Protestant and Catholic alike; and it was one on which the peace of Ireland, both North and South, could well depend.

References

1. Somerville and Ross, *The Irish R.M.* Complete, p. 7.
2. Appendix, speech on Sunningdale.
3. Terence O'Neill, *Autobiography*, p. 86.
4. Henry Fairlie, *The Life of Politics*, p. 84.
5. O'Hart, *Irish Pedigrees*, p. 49.
6. Maurice Craig, *Dublin*, p. 203.
7. J. B. Doyle, *Tours in Ulster*.
8. N. Phillips Brown, *The Horse in Ireland*, p. 12.
9. S. E. Long, *Orangeism In Northern Ireland*, p. 1.
10. S. E. Long, *Orangeism In Northern Ireland*, p. 3.
11. Belfast News-Letter, 12 July 1956.
12. NI Hansard, 23 June 1966.
13. Irish News, 13 August 1971.
14. House of Commons Debates (Westminster), vol. 150, col 1270, 16 February 1922.
15. Belfast News-Letter, 31 January 1949.
16. Belfast News-Letter, 31 January 1949.
17. Appendix, speech on Sunningdale.
18. Appendix, Maiden Speech.
19. NI Hansard, 8 June 1960.
20. NI Hansard, 22 June 1960.
21. NI Hansard, 11 May 1960.
22. NI Hansard, 25 November 1958.
23. NI Hansard, 14 February 1961.
24. NI Hansard, 26 April 1960.
25. NI Hansard, 26 October 1961.
26. NI Hansard, 13 February 1962.
27. NI Hansard, 23 October 1962.

28. NI Hansard, 7 April 1965.
29. NI Hansard, see Commerce Estimates speeches, 1964 and 1965, and W. R. Boyd MP.
30. Personal information.
31. Faulkner-O'Neill resignation letters, January, 1969.
32. Terence O'Neill, *Autobiography*, p. 40.
33. Conor Cruise O'Brien, *States of Ireland*, p. 170.
34. John Biggs-Davison, *The Hand is Red*, p. 141.
35. NI Hansard, 2 May 1967.
36. Terence O'Neill, *Autobiography*, p. 129.
37. Protestant Telegraph, 27 March 1971.
38. David Bleakley, *Peace in Ulster*, p. 100.
39. NI Hansard, 31 March 1971.
40. Cahal B. Daly, *Violence in Ireland*, p. 45.
41. NI Hansard, 5 October 1971.
42. NI Hansard, 5 October 1971.
43. Official Statement, 9 August 1971.
44. Statement on Peace, 29 August 1971.
45. Belfast Telegraph, 9 August 1971.
46. Joint statement by leaders of Protestant Churches, August 1971.
47. Irish News, 31 August 1971.
48. London Times, 27 September 1971.
49. Accounts of Unionism see: H. Kelly, *How Stormont Fell*, A. Boyd, *Brian Faulkner and the Crisis of Ulster Unionism*, J. F. Harbinson, *The Ulster Unionist Party, 1882/1973*.
50. Appendix, final message to Northern Ireland people.
51. Personal information.
52. Appendix, Bow Group lecture; also writings appendices A & C p. 154 and p. 168.
53. White Paper, NI Constitutional Proposals, March 1973; see, also, the Cameron Report NI (Cmd 532) 1969 and the Royal Commission on the Constitution (Cmnd 5460) 1973 for useful background information.
54. Appendix, Sunningdale Document.
55. See Belfast Telegraph, 29 May 1974.

APPENDIX 1

Selected Speeches

15 March 1949: Maiden Speech in Northern Ireland House of Commons

I have the greatest pleasure in rising to second the Motion which has been so ably and so adequately proposed by my right hon. Friend. In doing so, I am bound to say that he has covered the field very adequately, and if I indulge in a certain amount of repetition perhaps hon. Members will bear with me, as it is my maiden effort.

I rise for two reasons. First of all, the closing of the branches mentioned in the County Down Railway would seriously affect many of my constituents in East Down. Secondly, I feel that the future welfare of Ulster is at stake. I feel that either of those two reasons would be sufficient to justify my intervention in the Debate. The right hon. Gentleman who moved this Motion quoted from the speech by the Minister of Commerce during the Second Reading of the Bill last June. I would merely read one or two lines of that speech. The Minister on that occasion said, with reference to the proposal of the directors to close down these parts of the County Down Railway:

> I had to tell them that I could not approve of such action, and indeed that I should be bound to do all in my power to prevent it . . . It would, moreover, have deprived many people in County Down of transport services which are essential to them, although they may not be profitable to the company.— (*Official Report*, 2nd June, 1948, *Vol.* 32, *Col.* 1888.)

I am encouraged by the sentiments which the Minister expressed on that occasion, because I feel that conditions are exactly the same to-day, and that, therefore, he must view with some alarm, as I and many others do, the closing down of certain lines as is now suggested by the Ulster Transport Authority. It is a well-known fact that, with the exception of the Bangor line, the railway has for several reasons been losing money for years. Traffic has been falling off as a result of competition from road transport which is now intensified. The rolling-stock of the company has not been maintained and improved in line with modern developments, because the company had not adequate funds to do so, but people generally had high hopes that the co-ordination of road and rail transport would mean that the railway would be developed in a modern way.

Now, what do they find? They find that co-ordination, as translated by the Ulster Transport Authority, means cancellation. To my mind this abandonment of the main line would be a fatal step. It is a course which would suggest itself to men whose only interest was road transport. I hope, indeed I am sure, that the executive of the Ulster Transport Authority are not men with one-track minds of that kind. It is obviously the easiest course, the course which requires the minimum of thought, of energy, of foresight and of initiative. I feel certain that those same executives are not men of that easy-going calibre.

The decision to close a railway is rather like the decision to cut down a tree. Once the crosscut has done its work there is no going back on it. Are there not means by which traffic could be attracted to the railway? First of all, if we assume that the existing rolling stock is inefficient, would it not be feasible to introduce a system of Diesel rail cars? In order to attract bulk passenger traffic would it not be worth while to introduce a system of reduced season tickets for men who travel in such large numbers to Belfast, particularly to the Queen's Island every day?

During the past few days I have been besieged with letters, telegrams and telephone calls from people who travel on various branches of the railway to their work day by day, but particularly by people—I am bound to mention them—who travel on the ten minutes to seven train in the morning from Ballynahinch Junction. Those people have been using the railway for years. They are mainly the salt of the earth—the men who work at the Queen's Island. There are also large numbers of young ladies who travel in on that train to work in offices in Belfast. If they are to be deprived of that service in the morning it will be most difficult for them to get to their work.

At present the railway is not supported at certain times of the day. Would it not then be worth while to cut down the services and to concentrate them on the rush hours and busy times? At present also, there is a considerable duplication of depots and offices, et cetera, by the Transport Authority and by the railway. Would it not be possible to amalgamate road and rail staffs in the same premises? It may be argued that to continue the railway it must be subsidised, but even if we accept this provision we are not breaking new ground, because it is a well-known fact that there are many unremunerative bus routes in Ulster, and that those routes are kept going by the bus routes which pay well. Successive Governments have argued this principle in favour of the road transport system. We have been told that private enterprise could not give such a service on unremunerative routes, but that a public utility company could and would. Surely the Ulster Transport Authority is a public utility.

If I might draw the memory of hon. Members back to a time many years ago when the shipyards at the Queen's Island were in danger of closing down—there was grass growing on many of the slipways—the late Lord Craigavon in his wisdom, and using the great commonsense which he possessed as an Ulsterman, realised that the shipyards must not close down. What did he do? He subsidised British shipping companies; he loaned them the money in order to build ships and keep the shipyards working, and the result was shown to us in 1939 when the most efficient shipyards in the world were available for building ships of the King's navy and ships of the King's merchant marine. I feel that the same argument applies to the Belfast and County Down Railway.

Freight services will be particularly affected in my area by any closing of the railway, because obviously there are advantages in the carrying of certain classes of merchandise by a railway. I am thinking of one particular instance. The East Downshire Steamship Company brings a steamer into Dundrum once a week. That steamer has a cargo of 400 tons of coal. It has to discharge its cargo and turn round in the course of one tide. It is able to do that because the Belfast and Down Railway provides a number of waggons on the quay sufficient to take the whole cargo and distribute it to areas all over east Down. If that service were in the hands of lorries it would take between 80 and 100 lorries to handle it in the time. In the first place I do not believe the lorries would be available, and if they were available there would be ground for criticism because obviously they could not be kept busy all the time.

Many classes of heavy freight are more suited to rail than to road transport. Seed potatoes from the Mourne district are shipped to the docks at Belfast, and last year 5,000 tons of seed potatoes were carried by the Belfast and County Down Railway from Newcastle to Belfast. It does not require a great deal of imagination to conceive the amount of congestion there would be at the docks if those potatoes were brought in by lorries to Belfast. I could quote many individual examples of freight that is handled by the company, but rather than weary the House by doing so I will content myself with quoting three figures which, I believe, will be of interest. They are taken from the war years—times of stress during which, as my right hon. Friend (Mr. Andrews) said, those in authority appreciated the value of this railway.

In the year 1941 the Belfast and County Down railway carried practically one-third of the number of passengers carried by the Road Transport Board all over Ulster; the railway carried 11,000,000 passengers and the Road Board 39,000,000. In 1940 the railway carried one-tenth of the freight tonnage handled by the Road Transport Board all over Ulster, and in the same year, 1940, the railway carried one-fifth of the total head of cattle carried by the Transport Board in all the areas of Ulster. Everyone will agree that the dread of war is still present, and any decision affecting the future of this railway should, I feel, be made, and made most seriously, with that in mind. I said earlier that I felt the future welfare of Ulster was at stake. This House has voted large sums of money towards tourist development. Is the railway not an essential link in the chain of tourist attraction?

Admittedly it has not played its full part in the past, but there is no reason why it should not have a greater function now and in the future. Supposing, for instance, and it is not a wild conjecture, that a holiday village was established at Bishopscourt, near Ardglass, it would be an ideal situation for such a village. What better place could there be than Bishopscourt or some such place in East Down to set up a holiday village? The railway company could bring all the visitors to that holiday village direct from the ships where they landed at Belfast. It could bring all the provisions, the coal and the merchandise that would be required by the village. Surely the railway has an essential function to perform in relation to tourist development.

Hotel accommodation in Ulster is inadequate, every one agrees on that point. There are many places on the Belfast and County Down line where money could be well spent in building hotels, better spent, perhaps, than the £60,000 which it is stated the Transport Authority are spending, or have spent, on a derelict hotel building in the city of Derry, which is hardly likely to have any great tourist attraction.

Perhaps enough has been said to impress upon the Minister the feelings of the County Down people on this matter. I know that the final decision whether or not the line will be closed will not be with the Minister but with the Tribunal. I am sure, however, that the Transport Authority in putting their case to the Tribunal will be guided by the Minister's good advice. It is difficult for hon. Members to get through the College of Cardinals formed by the executives of the Transport Authority, and to get into the presence of the Pope himself, but perhaps the Minister is able to penetrate and get there. I would ask him—I would appeal to him—to impress upon the head of the Transport Authority the feelings of the people of County Down about the closing of this railway, and perhaps the Minister will get from him a pontiff's blessing for the future of the Belfast and County Down Railway. If the Minister does so he will be upholding the honour of Down.

24 March 1972: Final message as Prime Minister to the Northern Ireland people following the announcement of Direct Rule

On Wednesday Senator Andrews and I travelled to London for what we well knew would be a crucially important meeting with Mr Heath and his colleagues. We were determined to do anything we could reasonably do to restore peace and stability to Ulster and confident that we would hear from Mr Heath realistic proposals to help end the violence and find a new way forward for this community.

Even as we sat at the Cabinet table at 10 Downing Street, news reached me of yet another massive explosion in the centre of Belfast, with further casualties to innocent civilians who were once again the victims of foul and callous terrorism. We were deeply conscious, too, of the appalling situation in such places as Londonderry, a city of the United Kingdom which includes enclaves of total lawlessness, from which come those who day and daily wreck more and more of the business and commercial centre of that city.

Our objective—and I had hoped the objective of the whole United Kingdom—was to end this violence, to end it completely, and to end it once and for all. We went to Downing Street fully prepared to acknowledge that, in defeating the violence, military means would have to be buttressed by *realistic* political proposals, designed to unite the communities and detach them from any sympathy or support for violent men. We had indeed, in a comprehensive letter, made such proposals ourselves to the United Kingdom Government.

But I was faced at the Cabinet table not with a wide-ranging review of all these aspects, or with a comprehensive, coherent and final "package" of proposals—which we ourselves had suggested—but with the idea of a constitutional Referendum and some movement on internment, both of which we found perfectly acceptable, and firm proposals to appoint a Secretary of State and to transfer to Westminster vital and fundamental powers which we have exercised for over half a century. The proposition put to us was that all statutory and executive responsibility for law and order should be vested in the United Kingdom Parliament and Government. These included criminal law and procedure (including the organisation of and appointments to the courts); public order; prisons and penal establishments; the creation of new penal offences; special powers; the public prosecuting power, and the police. Even these radical changes were simply to pave the way for further, entirely open-ended discussion, with continuing speculation and uncertainty as we have seen it in recent weeks.

I asked, naturally, whether the drastic proposal to transfer security powers was rooted in any conviction on their part that we had abused these powers. It was made clear to me that no such suggestion was made; that this diminution in the powers, prestige and authority of Stormont was in reality simply a response to the criticism of our opponents, which Mr Heath and his colleagues neither substantiated nor supported.

Of course, chief amongst those who have sought the emasculation and ultimately the downfall of Stormont have been the IRA terrorists themselves. And when it was made clear to me that the United Kingdom Government could not give an assurance of any further positive measures against terrorism, I felt bound to ask whether the end of violence was being sought, not—as we have always asserted—by defeating the terrorists, but by surrendering to them.

Nevertheless, because we fully realised the gravity of all the issues at stake, we expressed a willingness to identify areas of security policy in which the United Kingdom Government could reasonably expect a more effective voice. Chief amongst these was internment policy. The operation of detaining men for internment depends largely on the use of troops, and the United Kingdom Government is responsible internationally for the defence of the policy—as for example, by derogation from the European Human Rights Convention. Recognising this joint interest, we offered to make future decisions, both on new internments and on a policy for releases, joint decisions. Moreover, in an attempt to begin a de-escalation of the entire situation, we offered to make an immediate gesture by way of the release of certain internees of a lower risk category, with further releases dependent upon a matching response.

It was made clear to us, however, that the United Kingdom Cabinet at its meeting next day was likely to re-affirm the decision to transfer all law and order responsibilities. I then informed Mr Heath and his colleagues that, as I had stated publicly on many previous occasions, the Government of Northern Ireland would not accept such a situation. I told him that it would be widely construed as an acceptance of totally baseless criticism of our stewardship; that it would be seen by the IRA and others as a first and major step on the road to a terrorist victory; and that it would leave the Government of Northern Ireland bereft of any real influence and authority by removing the most fundamental power of any Government. I said clearly that we were not interested in maintaining a mere sham, or a face-saving charade.

Yesterday morning, we reported this situation to our respective Cabinets. Our colleagues here affirmed with complete unanimity that stand which Senator Andrews and I had taken; and in the early afternoon Mr Heath telephoned me to say that the British Cabinet found our counter-proposals unacceptable, and re-affirmed their earlier decision to transfer law and order powers. In view of the gravity of this position, he invited us to return at once to London for a further discussion.

Last night, at 10 Downing Street, I handed to Mr Heath a letter signed by all of those who were present at our Cabinet meeting, and endorsed by those members of the Government who were not present. It is quite brief and I will read it to you:
"Dear Prime Minister

You have just conveyed to us by telephone the decision of the United Kingdom Cabinet that all responsibilities of the Northern Ireland Government and Parliament in relation to law and order should be transferred to Westminster. You have also made it clear that even this change is intended only to create a situation in which further radical changes, of a nature we believe to be unrealistic and unacceptable, will be discussed.

We now convey to you formally the unanimous view of the Cabinet of Northern Ireland that such a transfer is not justifiable and cannot be supported or accepted by us. It would wholly undermine the powers, authority and standing of this Government without justification and for no clear advantage to those who are suffering in Northern Ireland today.

We wish to point out with a sense of the heavy responsibility involved that the imposition of this proposal, involving as it will the resignation of the Government of Northern Ireland as a whole, may have the gravest consequences, the full extent of which cannot now be foreseen."

Mr Heath told us that, in view of our decision, he would propose to announce at Westminster today a temporary suspension of our devolved institutions of Government, under which the Stormont Parliament would be prorogued and a Bill would be introduced to vest the powers of the Government of Northern Ireland, for the time being, in a Secretary of State. So that there would be no breach in the orderly government of the country, he asked if we would be willing to remain in office for a few days until this legislation had become effective—a request which I felt it my duty to meet. Mr Heath has now made this statement at Westminster. It includes a proposal to nominate an Advisory Commission—a proposal which we oppose as basically undemocratic.

This is a serious and sad situation, reached after three years of the most strenuous efforts to reform our society on a basis at once fair and realistic. I thought that by our actions and our attitude we had earned the right to the confidence and the support of the United Kingdom Government. I fear, too, that many people will draw a sinister and depressing message from these events:—that violence *can* pay; that violence *does* pay; that those who shout, lie, denigrate and even destroy earn for themselves an attention that responsible conduct and honourable behaviour do not. They may ask—if Belfast is to bow to violence today—where will it be next year? Birmingham? Glasgow? London?

But I give this message to the people of Northern Ireland. We in the Government have preferred to give up our offices rather than surrender what we regard as a vital principle. We have had a grave disagreement with the United Kingdom Government, but we have endeavoured to conduct that disagreement with dignity, and in the way which will least damage the Ulster we love and the United Kingdom as a whole. I ask all our people—concerned as they are bound to be—also to have regard to what is vital, and to behave always with dignity. We will continue to assert and defend in other lawful ways the legitimate interests of the great majority of Ulster people. And so I ask our people at this difficult and trying time to remain calm and on no account to be led by unwise agitation into any possible confrontation with the security forces, which have been making such tremendous sacrifices on our behalf. We will work, with total determination and utter firmness, but responsibly and under the law, to ensure that the voice of the Ulster majority— which is not a sectarian majority, but a majority of responsible people loyal to the Crown—is heard loud and clear throughout the land.

14 December 1973: Speech to the Northern Ireland Assembly on his return from the Sunningdale Conference

MR FAULKNER: Within this Chamber in the last 52 or 53 years I have no doubt that many important documents have been discussed. I am quite convinced that never in that time has any document with so much potential for good in it for the Ulster community been discussed.

HON. MEMBERS: Nonsense.

MR FAULKNER: A lot of people have talked about the difficulties of Sunningdale. Some have questioned the achievements of Sunningdale.

MR POOTS: You are not joking.

MR FAULKNER: I believe that the real achievement of Sunningdale was the fact that in the short term it has created conditions in which violence and fear just cannot survive in Northern Ireland.

MR POOTS: What are you talking about?

MR FAULKNER: There is not a man or a woman representing constituencies in this Assembly who has not got constituents at the moment that are living in fear — —

MR HUTCHINSON: And anger.

MR FAULKNER: — — and are suffering from violence. Sunningdale has in the short term created the conditions in which neither of these things can survive. No matter what it may cost any of us in our political future the days spent at Sunningdale were from my point of view well worthwhile.

MR POOTS: Nonsense.

MR FAULKNER: But more than that I believe — —

MR MCQUADE: You gave the country away.

MR FAULKNER: that in the long term —

MR MCQUADE: You gave the country away.

MR FAULKNER — — Sunningdale has created conditions in which not only can there be greater economic prosperity — —

MR HUTCHINSON: Nonsense.

MR FAULKNER — — in the whole island of Ireland — —

AN HON. MEMBER: Rubbish.

MR FAULKNER — — but there can be a real bond of friendship not just between the people North and South but between the Governments North and South, which is essential if a real friendship between the peoples North and South is to flourish as it has not done in 53 years. If we recognise that this is an achievement, how has it been brought about?

MR JAMES CRAIG: So was the Hunt Report a great achievement.

MR FAULKNER: I was very impressed with what Mr Hume said earlier this evening.

HON MEMBERS: Oh. [*Interruption.*]

MR SPEAKER: Order, order. We have had a very good and temperate debate and I think that everyone has had that privilege of speaking without interruption. I would ask hon. Members to give Mr Faulkner the right to make his statement without undue interruption.

MR JAMES CRAIG: Mr Speaker, no one threw Mr Faulkner out today.

MR FAULKNER: And nobody will in the future either.

MR POOTS: You are on a precipice.

MR MCQUADE: You are not very far from it.

MR FAULKNER: What impressed me particularly in the middle of, if I may say it in the presence of this Assembly, an excellent speech from Mr Hume, was that he said — —

MRS PAISLEY (East Belfast): You are blacking his boots.

MR FAULKNER — — that the decisions that had been taken had been taken without any sacrifice of principle on anybody's part.

HON. MEMBERS: Oh, ho.

MR FAULKNER: You see it is so easy to laugh. It is the best possible indication — —

MR MCQUADE: On a point of order.

MR FAULKNER — — of the paucity of brains and the over-abundance of — —

MR MCQUADE: On a point of order.

MR FAULKNER — — noise.

MR MCQUADE: I want to silence the noise. We have nothing else to give away. You have given the country away. That is the last thing — —

MR SPEAKER: That is not a point of order.

MR MCQUADE: You have given the country away. What else is there to give away?

MR SPEAKER: Mr Faulkner.

MR FAULKNER: I think that the means of achievement were found at Sunningdale because people were able to get together and work together without in any way — —

MR BURNS: Singing together.

MR FAULKNER — — sacrificing their ideals, which reflected con-flicting aspirations. They were able to accept each other's rights to hold their ideals and yet agree to work together for the welfare of the community in which they lived. You are going to see a lot more of that, Mr Speaker, over the next four years if I am not very much mistaken. Now let me detail the means that were used to bring about these achievements.

MR HUTCHINSON: Traitors' achievement.

MR FAULKNER: First of all the British Government, the Irish Government, and the members of the Northern Ireland Executive-to-be accepted in full all — —

MR POOTS: To be, you can say that again.

MR FAULKNER — — the terms of the Constitution Act of 1973. We recognised that there were a number of obligations within that Act. The first was that there could be no change wrought in the Constitution of Northern Ireland by this Assembly or by Parliament at Westminster because Parliament at Westminster had wisely put the matter firmly in the hands of the people of Northern Ireland.

HON MEMBERS: Oh, ho.

MR FAULKNER: We accepted that. Secondly, we accepted that they having done that, they had also put an obligation upon the people of Northern Ireland that there could only be a regional Government in Northern Ireland if people representing the varying interests of those that sent them to the Assembly could get together and form that Government. Now then, sitting down at Sunningdale last week, we established that the Irish Government were prepared to accept the status of Northern Ireland and so were the British Government, and two declarations to that effect from those two Governments will be registered at the United Nations and will become an international Agreement.

MR JAMES CRAIG: What about Article 2?

MR FAULKNER: The people who talk such a lot — —

MR JAMES CRAIG: You are the man who said it had to be removed.

MR FAULKNER — — about the 1925 Agreement about the League of Nations, quite honestly display their ignorance of the League of Nations and Article 2 because in the first place the League of Nations was no more like the United Nations of today — —

PROFESSOR LINDSAY: That is untrue.

MR FAULKNER — — than this Assembly was like the Parliament of Patagonia, and I do not know anything about the Parliament of Patagonia.

MR MCQUADE: Well, it is you who is talking about it.

MR FAULKNER: This declaration from these two Governments has provided the confidence for the people of Northern Ireland to do their best to see that our institutions of government work.

MR MCQUADE: That is what you are — —

MR SPEAKER: Order, Order. I must ask hon. Members to show tolerance in the Chamber. I will probably have to take stronger action in future against anyone who disregards what I say.

MR MCQUADE: Thank you, Mr Speaker. I could not listen to any more of that.

Mr McQuade withdrew from the Chamber.

MR FAULKNER: We have created institutions of government which enable not just the SDLP opposite but I believe the political minority as a whole in Northern Ireland, I believe, a majority of the citizens of the Republic to identify themselves with the institutions of government in Northern Ireland. If we had achieved that many years ago we would have had a much healthier society in Ulster today. Let me go into one or two of the things which have brought about — —

MR HUTCHINSON: Go into Long Kesh.

MR FAULKNER — — this state of affairs. We have heard talk outside this House and inside it this evening about the Council of Ministers — —

MR BURNS: You will not go back to the people and have it confirmed.

MR FAULKNER — — in the Council of Ireland. Whatever

anybody's idealistic notions may be about a Council of Ireland he must surely recognise the possibility of practical results from such a Council. I doubt whether there is anybody in this House, no matter what his or her political label, who could go back to his or her constituency and say, "I resisted means whereby the police in the North and the police in the South could get together to catch terrorists." Yet that is just what can be done through the Council of Ireland. I doubt very much whether there is —— —

MR DUNLOP (Mid-Ulster): Will the hon. Member give way?

MR FAULKNER: I will not give way, no.

MR DUNLOP: You would give way to the other fellows.

MR FAULKNER: I doubt very much whether there is anybody in this House who could go back to his constituents this evening and say that he resisted measures that would bring about legal action against fugitives from violence in Northern Ireland. I doubt whether there is anybody in this House who could go back to his constituents and get any satisfaction from them if he said: "We resisted means for better economic co-operation between North and South."

MR BURNS: We had that. Surely we had that. That is not new.

MR FAULKNER: Had you indeed? I do not see much evidence of it. There is certainly not a Unionist in this House who could go back to his constituents tonight and say — [*Interruption.*] —

MR SPEAKER: Order, order. For the last time I warn hon. Members that I am going to demand the freedom of speech that they are always requesting for other people. Please let Mr Faulkner finish his speech. You will all have an opportunity of making your own speeches. I would ask you to give him a chance to make his speech.

REV. DR PAISLEY: On a point of order, Mr Speaker. Surely if a Member refuses to give way when he is asked to do so he only invites people to interject. If the hon. Member were willing to give way and let a proper question be put to him it would avoid these interjections.

MR DEVLIN: That is not a point of order.

AN HON. MEMBER: It would keep order in the Assembly.

MR HUME: On your terms.

REV. DR PAISLEY: Mr Speaker, I am waiting for you to give a Ruling, not for the hon. Gentleman opposite.

MR DEVLIN: It is not a point of order.

REV. DR PAISLEY: I want to add to that point of order and to say that when hon. Members on this side were speaking and were interrupted by hon. Members opposite, including the hon. Member who is now yapping, they did not complain. We have now defence from the other side instead of being properly defended by the Chair.

MR SPEAKER: Order, order.

MR CURRIE: Sit down.

MR SPEAKER: Order, order.

REV. DR PAISLEY: I will not sit down.

MR SPEAKER: Order, order.

REV. DR PAISLEY: I will not. I will not sit down for Mr Currie.

MR SPEAKER: Order, order. Dr. Paisley. Order, order.

REV. DR PAISLEY: Get them in order.

MR DEVLIN: Throw him out.

MR CURRIE: Stop yapping.

REV. DR PAISLEY: If you get them to sit down—

MR SPEAKER: I ask you to sit down or to withdraw from the House.

REV. DR PAISLEY: When they keep quiet.

MR SPEAKER: You will either sit down or withdraw from the House.

REV. DR PAISLEY: Is that so?

MR SPEAKER: That is quite so.

HON. MEMBERS: Oh.

REV. DR PAISLEY: Then rebuke them on the other side. [*Interruption.*]

MR POOTS: What about fair play for us?

MR SPEAKER: Under the Standing Orders which Members on all sides passed I will rebuke any Member on any side of the House who offends. Standing Order 40 (3,*e*) refers to a Member who 'persistently and wilfully disregards the authority of the Speaker.' All I am asking from both sides is for freedom of speech in this Chamber. Surely that is not too much. Mr Faulkner.

MR FAULKNER: Thank you, Mr Speaker. You and I have been Members of this House longer than most people and, if you are as little worried about the verbal diarrhoea as I am, then we will get on all right.

HON. MEMBERS: Oh.

HON. MEMBERS: Oh.

AN HON. MEMBER: A dirty one.

MR FAULKNER: Yes, it is a dirty one. What I was saying before I was—I suppose you could call it 'interrupted'—was that there are surely no Unionists in this Assembly who could go home to their constituents and say, 'We resisted a Unionist veto on these organizations that are going to bring so much benefit to the people of Northern Ireland.'

MR BURNS: That is not a new one.

MR FAULKNER: If people look at the Sunningdale Agreement carefully they will see that we have achieved what has been missing for generations, namely, respect and support—

MR BARR: On a point of order.

MR FAULKNER: from everybody in Northern Ireland—

MR BARR: On a point of order.

HON. MEMBERS: A point of order.

MR FAULKNER — for the forces of — —

—MR. BARR: After the Sunningdale Conference Mr Hume said on television—

MR DEVLIN: That is not a point of order.

MR BARR: Shut your mouth.

MR DEVLIN: It is not a point of order.

MR POOTS: Shut that big mouth.

MR BARR: He said that not only have the Unionists got the veto but so also have the SDLP and the Alliance Party. Am I right or wrong, Mr Hume?

MR HUME: Quite wrong.

MR SPEAKER: Mr Faulkner.

MR FAULKNER: Mr Speaker, I doubt whether there is anybody in the Assembly who would really have said before we went to Sunningdale, 'Those people are going to come back from Sunningdale' — —

MR BARR: With nothing.

MR FAULKNER — — 'with a commitment from the British Government to restore responsibility for the RUC and for law and order to the Assembly.'

MR POOTS: That is not right.

MR FAULKNER: There are lots of people talking about it now; nobody was talking about it before. Let it be clearly understood that those of us in the Executive, all the parties in the Executive, will be very anxious to see that Ulster people are responsible for peace when they are trying to be responsible for good government.

MR BURNS: Responsible for a united Ireland.

MR FAULKNER: The discussions have also provided for immediate legal action against fugitives from violence and immediate action against murderers.

MR DUNLOP: Will the hon. Member give way for five minutes, please?

MR FAULKNER: No, I will not give way for five minutes at all.

I did not interrupt anybody. I sat without saying a word until I got up on my feet to speak and I am not prepared to give way to you or to anybody else.

AN HON. MEMBER: You gave way to Republicans.

MR FAULKNER: If you have a point of order I will have to give way; otherwise I will not give way.

I think it was Mr Bleakley who said that there was not sufficient Anglo-Irish dimension in this Agreement. I believe there was one very important Anglo-Irish dimension and that was the commitment by the Governments in Dublin and London to establish at once a commission to go into the whole question of extradition and common law enforcement. That is being done at this moment. If it had been done four years ago we might have avoided a great deal of the violence we have already seen. [*Interruption.*]

MR JAMES CRAIG: You are a lig.

MR FAULKNER: I do not believe that anybody in this House could go home to his constituents and say that there was something wrong in an Agreement which provided the means by which the Chief Constable of the RUC and the Commissioner of the *Gardai* could sit down together to find out ways to deal with violence on an all-Ireland basis. My goodness, if the people who 'Tut, tut' now had been able to have had this done four years ago we might have stemmed the violence at birth, we might have prevented the Army from coming here at all and we might have saved hundreds of lives.

MR DUNLOP: On a point of clarification.

MR FAULKNER: We have got to recognize——

MR DUNLOP: A point of clarification.

MR SPEAKER: Order, order.

MR FAULKNER —— that all of this is only possible because three parties have come together to form what amounts to a Coalition Government. I recognize —— ——

MR POOTS: You are not a Unionist any longer.

MR FAULKNER —— that there are thousands of Ulstermen and women who felt a very serious shock at the loss of the old Stormont Parliament and I confess that I was amongst them.

MR POOTS: You made a poor job of getting it back.

MR FAULKNER: As a result of all that there are many Ulstermen and women—probably thousands of them—who are suspicious of any new proposals for government in Northern Ireland because, if we are to be honest —— ——

MR BURNS: You are not suspicious.

MR FAULKNER — — thousands of people in Ulster have completely lost confidence in politics. I believe that it ought to be the determination of all of us to get confidence restored to political institutions. We are not going to do that by repeating the scenes that have been enacted in this Assembly since it started to operate. We are not going to achieve it by going around the country squabbling with one another about the way in which the country is run from here while the country is perhaps stagnating economically.

I sympathize with the attitude of people who feel this way. I want to speak directly to them tonight and to say with all the conviction at my command that I do not believe any principles have been lost. I consider that all our principles are firmly protected in the new institutions. What is more, for the first time all the people of Northern Ireland can identify with those institutions and can look to them with confidence in the future. For almost two years we have had no regional Government at all. Now we are going to have what I can say will be a very strong and determined team in Government.

AN HON. MEMBER: Nonsense.

REV. WILLIAM BEATTIE: There will be IRA men in it.

MR FAULKNER: We are going to have a team — —

MR HUTCHINSON: Sit down. Since the days of Lundy you are the biggest Lundy we have ever seen. That is all you are.

MR SPEAKER: Order, order.

MR FAULKNER: We shall have a team in Government which will not tolerate violence.

AN HON. MEMBER: That will be something new.

AN HON. MEMBER: Have a bit of sense.

MR FAULKNER: We shall have a team in Government — —

MR CURRIE: Would the right hon. Member give way?

MR FAULKNER — — which will promote a social and economic programme which will not only be energetic but will be effective for every section of our community — —

MR HUTCHINSON: Sit down.

MR FAULKNER — — because it will be a programme which comes with the united determination — —

MRS DICKSON: On a point of order. It is very difficult for Members on this side of the House to hear what is being said.

AN HON. MEMBER: Ask the speaker to speak up.

MRS DICKSON: In the past we have heard a great deal about democratic principles. Let us see them in practice and at least listen to the point of view which is being put forward.

151

REV. DR PAISLEY: Let the right hon. Member give way, as everybody does. [*Interruption.*]

MRS DICKSON: On a further point of order. Surely it is customary to give way to one Member, but not to 10 or 12 at a time.

REV. DR PAISLEY: He has not given way to one person.

MR FAULKNER: I said earlier, Mr. Speaker, that you and I have been Members of this House for longer, I believe, than any other Members. In the almost 25 years that I have been here I have received both brickbats and commendations. I mean it honestly when I say that since the decision to establish the Executive and since our return from the Sunningdale Conference I have received more commendations than in the previous 25 years. [*Interruption.*] I invite the Members who are shouting to take a walk along Royal Avenue, up the Shankill Road or up the Falls Road—[*Interruption.*] On a point of order. Is Mr Faulkner prepared to go to the country to test the statement he has just made?

REV. WILLIAM BEATTIE: It is a good point.

MR FAULKNER: Mr Speaker, I think a dictionary on points of order would help these people. [*Interruption.*]

MR SPEAKER: Order, order. I personally am unable to hear the debate. I am ashamed of the noise that is being created in the Chamber by talking on both sides. Is it too much to ask Members to allow Mr Faulkner to finish his address in freedom and decency? Surely that is not asking too much. If Members wish to make any comments they should reserve them until they are speaking themselves.

MR MILLAR: Mr Speaker, would you remind his own team to shut their mouths, too? They are doing it.

MR SPEAKER: I ask you, sir, just to behave yourself.

MR MILLAR: Very good, Mr Speaker, but remind them, too. Tell them to shut up.

MR SPEAKER: Order, order. I have warned both sides of the House about the noise that is being made.

MR MILLAR: This side goes a wee bit further than where I am sitting.

MR SPEAKER: If you offend against me again I will you put out of the House. Mr Faulkner.

REV. DR PAISLEY: Use the jackboot.

MR FAULKNER: The Member who has just said: 'Use the jackboot' has given the people some advice in recent days. I understand he told them to go out into the highways and byways and hamlets and see what there would be. What did he mean? I say, 'Go out into the highways and byways; go into the hamlets; go into the cities, go into the towns. The one thing you will hear on all people's lips is this—"Good luck to you, gentlemen; make the institutions of government work at Stormont; give us good government again." ' I can say on behalf of the men who have agreed to work together on the Executive that Members are going to get good government. If they do not support it they can go to their constituents. Somebody asked me, 'What about an election?' I would welcome a General Election next month. I would take part in it with absolute confidence—

REV. WILLIAM BEATTIE: Adjourn the House and let us go to the country.

MR FAULKNER — knowing full well that the people will support us in what we are doing. [*Interruption*] One has to have regard for the people. They have already given their democratic opinion on at least two occasions this year—at the Border poll and the Assembly election.

REV. WILLIAM BEATTIE: Con man.

MR FAULKNER: Those of us who have consistently stuck to our policies in the Assembly election and since are now about to give the people the good government for which they asked. We will only ask that that government should be judged—[*Interruption.*]

MR SPEAKER: Order, order. I consider the noise that is being created a grave discourtesy to myself as Speaker. I ask Members personally to please allow the debate to continue in normal decency. Mr Faulkner.

MR FAULKNER: I firmly believe that the people will judge the Members who have been returned here on their attitudes in this Assembly. Up to date I am very content that they should judge the SDLP, the Alliance Party and my party on our attitude, which is an attitude that will win the day, for every time other Members adopt irresponsible attitudes they are damaging institutions of government and bringing disrepute on themselves. There is talk about unity in this party and that party. Why cannot we unite on behalf of all the people—

REV. WILLIAM BEATTIE: It is a united Ireland you want.

MR FAULKNER—to take Ulster forward to peace, order and good Government? That is what I shall do, irrespective of political results.

REV. WILLIAM BEATTIE: The man who crawled out from under the stones has just spoken.

APPENDIX 2

Writings

1971: 'Ireland Today', an article published in *Aquarius*, the annual review of the priests and brothers of the Servite Order, Benburb, Co. Tyrone

Anyone who writes about the Irish political scene is immediately open to one of two charges: if he is an uninvolved outsider he is told that he does not know our problems intimately enough and that Irish politics are an art form only understood and appreciated after long years of study, and even then only by those born to it; if he is an Irishman, particularly one active in the political arena, he is told that he is biased. While there would seem to be no compromise solution to this problem of *critique*, there is nevertheless no lack of either category of commentator, and in joining the fray I am quite happy to be numbered amongst those who are directly involved in Irish politics. I say that not only because I am frequently appalled at the shallowness, insensitivity and naivety of many of the so-called "in depth" studies I have read of our situation, but also because I am convinced that direct participation in the politics of Northern Ireland is to-day especially worthwhile.

I shall declare my interest right away by saying that in my opinion the Unionist Government in which I have the honour to serve is making a major contribution to the well-being of this country, not merely through individual items of policy, but through the fundamental realism which is at the basis of all these policies and which must, in time, present an even greater challenge to all other political thinking in Ireland, both North and South.

It must be recognised that whatever way you look at 'the Irish problem' you are confronted with issues more emotional than rational. At one end of the scale the essence of the problem has been described in almost ethnic terms—the Planter and the Gael; the extension of this is the all too familiar 'explanation' in terms of religious divisions and antipathies; at the other end of the scale there are those who see the situation simply in terms of power blocks, on both sides of the border, with the supporters of ruling parties desperately defending their position. All these theories and their myriad mutations are, of course, over-simplifications. But what they all point to, in one way or another, is the existence of widespread, and underlying, emotional group identification.

Emotion by itself is not necessarily a negative force. Indeed, in political and national life, as in the life of the individual, it is a very necessary element. Poor indeed would be the man or the country devoid of emotional reactions and emotional energies, for in positive form they can be the motivating force for the humane actions of the individual and the idealism of a community. But where emotional identification becomes too pronounced—and it is my submission that this is the case in Ireland—the main danger is that political objectivity suffers: goals are pursued single-mindedly, even passionately, without enough thought as to how they fit into the over-all situation beyond the confines of one's own cherished ideals. In extreme cases reality is viewed through the prism of doctrinaire theories.

To see what one wants to see is not a peculiarly Irish intellectual vice, but we have perhaps more persistently given ourselves over to it than most other countries, to the point where our vision can be not only tinted but seriously blurred.

That is why I stress the need for political realism in Ireland to-day. And I wish to emphasize what I mean by that word, for too often when people have called for realism in dealing with problems in Ireland they have meant that our situation should be looked at phenomenologically: that is to say, looked at '*as it is*', as it would instantly confront a visitor with no knowledge of the country's background. Only in this way, the argument runs, can we ever get away from prejudice and divisions and make real progress. To me this view is not, however, realistic in the true sense of the word, for the history that has formed the present and, more especially, the deep awareness of that history, are, whether we like it or not, substantial factors which cannot be overlooked when we try to embrace the concept of 'Ireland'. For Ireland, like any other country, is not just a geographical location, not just a collection of cities and towns with a certain economy—it is above all the people who live there and their memories, allegiances and traditions which have formed differing and conflicting types of political consciousness. These are as much 'facts' about Ireland as the outline of our coasts traced upon a map. They loom large and will not simply go away through our choosing to ignore them. Having said that, I do acknowledge the terrible dangers of being imprisoned by the past and I most definitely believe in the need for everyone, particularly politicians, to face the facts of the present and the probable future and to examine, in the light of these facts, exactly where they are going and whether their own ideals are tenable.

It is right that I should look first of all at my own party and ask: What are the goals of Unionism in 1971? In many ways, they have not changed as regards fundamentals since Northern Ireland came into being—the constitutional link with the rest of the United Kingdom is still the cornerstone of our political philosophy. But there has developed over the years a new emphasis and, to a certain extent, new attitudes. While the Unionists of the early 1920's were understandably pre-occupied with the very survival of the new-born state and were working in conditions of extreme polarisation, Northern Ireland and Unionism have long since overcome the dangers of their political infancy. The 'stockade mentality' with which we used to be reproached rapidly changed as confidence in Northern Ireland as a political unit grew. To-day, the matter is beyond doubt: not only have the people of Northern Ireland shown their resolve to stay part of the United Kingdom at election after election over the past 50 years, but all the major parties at Westminster have publicly and unreservedly endorsed Northern Ireland's position. The full significance of this has perhaps not been generally appreciated, yet it is a development of major importance, since Westminster is, under the 1920 Government of Ireland Act, our parent Parliament, and this support right across the political spectrum there further underpins our position.

Within Northern Ireland the greatest single political factor to emerge over the years since partition—and one which provides the dynamic of the Unionism of the 70's, is that, economically, the case for Unionism has been proven in practice. Our understandable pride in this respect, our emphasis on higher living standards and the social security services which our population enjoy have often been held up to ridicule by our opponents and condemned as 'charity politics'; convenient clichés of abuse, such as 'subsidised statelet' have been used against us; and generally the impression given that Northern Ireland had sold its soul for the proverbial mess of pottage. But let us examine the factual position.

In the field of social welfare, embracing the Health services, benefit payments and education we are certainly greatly favoured, as compared with the Republic. For example, the per capita annual expenditure in Northern Ireland on the Health Service is £30, double the figure for the South. In education, we invest over £32 per head of population, as against £17 in the Republic. This is reflected in the number of pupils in post-Primary schools in Northern Ireland, which is proportionately double the Southern figure. And as for social welfare expenditure itself, the Republic spends £29 per head of population per annum, whereas Northern Ireland spends fully £71. It does not take an economist to grasp what these statistics mean in practical terms for families in both areas. Northern Ireland families are not only given better safeguards against the misfortunes of illness or unemployment and have better hospital services, their children also have much better educational opportunities to equip themselves with the skills and qualifications needed in modern society. Of course these great advantages are in large measure due to our membership of the United Kingdom. Of course we enjoy a net gain in terms of taxation raised deducted from total benefits. But this is the advantage which a small region, away from the centre, enjoys as part of a much larger whole, in any country. Within the context of the United Kingdom almost every region of Great Britain outside the South-East and the Midlands enjoys this sort of advantage. Again, the majority of the States of the German Federal Republic derive a similar gain from their membership of the Federation. How many *départements* in France 'pay their way'? Northern Ireland, like Scotland, the South-West or the North-East is entitled, as an integral part of the whole to enjoy this advantage and, on the other hand, to make valuable contributions to the life of the United Kingdom in terms of men, ideas and culture, as well as manufacturing production, in peace and in war.

The real barometer of Northern Ireland's economic health is, however, our trading figures. Our total trade in 1969—hardly a year in which an economist would have looked for freakishly favourable results—showed a further rise, to a new high of £1,400 million. Exports last year showed an increase of over 12 %, as compared with the previous year, which in turn had been a record year, with a rise of 17.5 %. All this points to the fact that the Northern Ireland economy is thriving and can stand on its own feet. And there is no explaining away the fact that in the industrial and commercial sphere we are doing proportionately three times as brisk a trade as our neighbours in the South.

So, quite apart from the welfare state benefits accruing to Northern Ireland, as a region of the United Kingdom, our economy has flourished and our standards of living are undeniably higher than those in the Republic. Personal income per capita in the North is one-third higher than in the Republic—a very sizeable gap for any two adjacent areas. Unionism has brought prosperity, and it is one of our major goals to develop this prosperity still further.

It is no secret that the troubles of the last two years have held us back from attaining the growth rate which could otherwise have been ours, but personally I am confident that in the long term we will see a greatly accelerated industrial expansion. Indeed, if actual growth rates in Western Europe over the next decade come anywhere near the present predictions, in the long-term Northern Ireland cannot lose. We have what it takes to be an attractive industrial location—our manufacturing tradition, a well trained labour force, and a well serviced country with an excellent infrastructure. The Five-Year Development Programme on which the Northern Ireland Government is at present embarked will further strengthen our position in this respect.

Increase in wealth, living standards and job opportunities are always desirable *per se*. But in the Northern Ireland context material development and improvements in amenities have a further significance, beyond their purely economic importance. For the provision of a good home for every family and a good job for every potential wage earner will certainly be a major factor in removing the discontent, fears and rivalries which have in the past, either in themselves or as catalysts, caused upheavals in our society. It is my personal belief that increased prosperity and good living conditions together will make up the biggest single factor in achieving permanent peace in Northern Ireland, for it is this sort of progress to which all men and women, regardless of political or religious affiliations, can reach out; it is this sort of progress which is of direct interest to every family in the land.

That is perhaps essentially a politician's view of the matter and I know that there are others who would place great emphasis on the importance, for example, of the ecumenical movement in reducing inter-denominational tensions. Undoubtedly, those who favour ecumenicity from a doctrinal point of view can justifiably feel that they are making a contribution towards blunting the edges of old animosities. But on the other side of the coin there is the danger of classifying as reactionary the many people, both Roman Catholic and Protestant, who sincerely reject this path for reasons of religious belief and personal conscience but who are nonetheless willing to practice good neighbourliness and to take part in co-operative actions in civic and public life. We must not look on any movement as the panacea for our problems—progress will come gradually and in many different ways, but I have no doubt that it will come.

I am not disguising for one moment the magnitude of the task which we face in Northern Ireland in eradicating community bitterness. But equally, we should not exaggerate the problem. Many visitors, led to believe that the two 'sides' in Northern Ireland were constantly at one another's throats, have been surprised to find that in everyday life the overwhelming majority of both persuasions are perfectly happy to work side by side, with mutual respect and understanding. All too often, we can become too introvertedly pre-occupied with our problems and allow them to get out of perspective. We must not forget that other countries have to deal with traditional divisions which run much deeper than ours—for example, the opposing linguistic groupings in Belgium, the balance of no less than three major cultural and national groups in Switzerland, not to mention the colour problems in so many countries in the world. It is the Unionist ideal to present a programme and to carry out policies which can benefit and politically appeal to every section of the community. This was never truer than it is to-day and despite the tensions of the recent past, anyone who makes a political prognosis purely on the basis of a counting of heads by religious affiliation is making an essentially sectarian assumption which is increasingly invalid.

Unionism is often attacked on the grounds that, as a political movement, it is 'unpatriotic' or at least schizophrenic, in that it asks Irishmen to be something more than Irishmen. I reject those charges utterly. The Scots can be Scottish *and* British, Englishmen can identify with both England *and* Britain. And in exactly the same way the Northern Ireland citizen is Irish *and* British; it is a question of complement, not of conflict. Indeed, in an age in which increasingly the Italians, the Germans and the Dutch, for instance, are looking on themselves as being Italians *and* Europeans, Germans *and* Europeans, Dutch *and* Europeans, the Unionist can feel himself already part of this trend of history.

While the Unionist identifies not only with Northern Ireland but with the United Kingdom as 'his country' he is to-day very much more aware of the historical background to Republican ideals. As we in Northern Ireland have moved away from the dangerous days of our foundation, we have been able to take a more mature and, with the perspective which only time can give, a more balanced view of what motivated Home Rulers and later Republicans. We recognise that historically the experience of the three centuries or so before partition was much harsher for the majority of the population in what is now Southern Ireland—absentee landlords, the Penal Code, the Great Famine and, by no means least, the rampant colonialism of the latter half of the 19th century, which saw in Irish demands for reforms the threat to Empire. Indeed, with hindsight it can be argued that, ironically, it was English Nationalism which prevented a satisfactory solution to the Irish question some 100 to 120 years ago. The subsequent history of this island might well have been happier, had a settlement been reached at that time. But there is no use our dreaming to-day of what might have been, and while Unionists appreciate why, in the past, many of their fellow Irishmen had good cause to look on England as 'the oul' enemy,' they feel that these animosities are not only outdated in themselves—as the vast majority of the citizens of the Republic would agree—but should have no part whatsoever in the political philosophies of the present.

It is not my business to criticise in detail the policies of political parties in the South—that is their affair. But insofar as these policies touch on Northern Ireland they are obviously of great interest to us and in general terms I would query whether the whole Republican ideal—in its many manifestations, across several party lines—is not outdated in the 1970s in many of its fundamental concepts, particularly in relation to Northern Ireland. To me much of the political philosophy in the South is still dominated by the 19th century ideal of independence. Sinn Feinism, in its emphasis on 'apartness' is the political fossil of this ideal and is widely recognised as such. But is not Republicanism in general, to which all political parties in the South must pay some sort of homage, still permeated with the myth of independence?

Let us pose the question: How independent is the Republic? In economic terms it is totally dependent on Britain, with which it does 80% of its trade. What would unemployment be like in the South if it were not for the exceptions to the Aliens Act and Commonwealth Immigration Act granted to her citizens? Rates of currency exchange are determined automatically by Britain, and how could the Republic's application for membership of the EEC be regarded separately from Britain's? Therefore, in the crassest terms, the Republic is utterly dependent on the United Kingdom. What would 'Irish freedom' be worth without the benevolence of the United Kingdom?—a benevolence, let it be emphasised, which has not been in doubt.

The more extreme elements of Republicanism tend to reject an economic emphasis on the grounds that this is a desertion of pure ideals, that it amounts to the 'worship of mammon,' and so on. I fully recognise the dangers of materialism in any society, but surely any patriotic ideal of freedom must, in the late 20th century, mean freedom in the sense of having the opportunity to lead a better way of life. Who can seriously suggest to-day that Britain is a colonial oppressor, either of the six counties or the twenty-six counties. What of the close on one million immigrants in Great Britain—are they enslaved? Surely the emotional issues of the past, which seem to me still to be amongst the main-springs of Republican philosophy, should fade in the light of economic realities. Is is not time for us in both parts of Ireland to pursue ideals which integrate economic and social, as well as emotional and cultural factors.

Northern Ireland has provided a useful diversion in the South away from economic questions: the 'problem of reunification,' being vague and obviously insoluble for the present, has proved to be all the more useful, for those very reasons, as a red herring in Southern politics.

As regards attitudes to the North, Republicanism has two main strands. First the moderate element, represented by Prime Minister Lynch, who hopes for a peaceful reunification by consent at some time in the future. Second, there are several small but militant groups, nowadays liberally sprinkled with Marxists and anarchists, who aim to overthrow existing political structures, both North and South, by force of arms.

The latter group, while their activities may be a thorn in the flesh, are no real danger, in that the population at large is only too well aware of the dictatorship they would try to impose. But Mr Lynch's brand of antipartitionism, which is no doubt sincere, though at times ill-informed, suffers from the same basic weakness—it is simply unrealistic. Given the growing importance of financial factors in political choice, how can any Republican politician expect that in the foreseeable future anything like a majority of Northern Ireland citizens would wish to throw in their lot with the Irish Republic and to break away from the United Kingdom?

It has been my position throughout this article to insist on realism. We have all, in Ireland, to live with facts—may we be preserved from 'solutionists' who ignore them! And when the basic fact is that at present, and as far as the political eye can see, Northern Ireland and Southern Ireland will pursue separate courses, then this fact must be squarely faced, with no pretence or wishful thinking. The main aim for Unionist and Republican alike should be on maximum development, economically and socially, for the benefit of the people of the two political areas. Progress is undoubtedly possible for both of us and it should not be sacrificed through unproductive upheaval or wranglings for the cause of an out-worn, emotional 'ideal.' What will become increasingly obvious in the future is that the ordinary citizen, both North and South, cares more for realities than symbols. Unionism is well prepared to meet the challenges which this growing preoccupation will bring forth.

10 April 1972: Paper on the Northern Ireland crisis read to the Conservative Bow Group

Those of us who have served Northern Ireland in Government at Stormont, have one overriding consideration in our minds at the present time: the well-being of the Ulster people. My colleagues and I, when we resigned two weeks ago, did so because we saw that we could not deflect the British Government from a course of action which we believed to be disastrous for our community.

We want peace for Northern Ireland as much—even more—than the British Government. Most of us have given a lifetime of service to making Ulster a better place to live in and in this we are the heirs of successive Unionist administrations which—in spite of the image of '50 years of Unionist misrule'—managed to produce a level of material prosperity for all citizens, irrespective of their politics, which would have been beyond the fondest hopes of those who set up the new state. We want peace. But it must be a fair peace, a just peace, a lasting peace.

We believe that our community faces a testing time under the administration of the new Secretary of State. It is our grave responsibility to see to it that the true interests of the people we represent—the overwhelming majority of the people of Ulster—are not overridden or overlooked. We believe, too, that our record in Government—acknowledged by Mr Heath and his colleagues—for fair dealing with the minority, entitles us to respect with the political opposition. During this unnecessary interregnum we shall do all in our power to advise the administration in Whitehall and Stormont in all things which we consider will bring back peace and prosperity to the Ulster people.

The British Government, however good their intentions might be, have not the knowledge that we have. They have not the sense of involvment that we have. They have not got our will to win. For Mr Heath and Mr Wilson and Mr Thorpe, the affairs of Northern Ireland are a matter of political science. You will understand that I do not exaggerate, when I say that for us in Ulster, it is a matter of life and death. It is understandable that people in Great Britain seeing our unfavourable reaction to Mr Heath's 'initiative' should ask: 'Why are Unionists opposed to direct rule?'

Firstly, let it be clear that the new arrangements for governing Northern Ireland are not direct rule, in that Ulster is not being administered in the same way as the rest of the United Kingdom. We are in a constitutional limbo, under-represented at Westminster, with much of the democratic processes of legislation effectively suppressed and a semi-colonial system of Government. I recognise, of course, that these are not intended to be permanent arrangements, but I would re-emphasise that my Party, which is by far the largest in Northern Ireland, and many other Parties, would find any prolongation of the arrangements beyond a single year to be unacceptable. Our aversion to the present set-up is surely understandable, but our attachment to Stormont goes far beyond such negative considerations. It is true that the founding fathers of Northern Ireland would have preferred to remain simply a region of the United Kingdom, administered directly from Westminster. But as the new state became established the advantages of a devolved Parliament and Government became more and more apparent. It was not only a question of our geography that made Stormont so useful—we were able, by exploiting our smaller scale of affairs to the full, to set up an administration which was efficient but was one of the most democratically accessible anywhere in the Western

World. Stormont was frequently—and in the past few years increasingly—attacked as the so called bastion of Protestant Ascendancy.

This is an allegation that I utterly reject and I have no doubt that every citizen in Northern Ireland will, in some way, at some time, over the next year, feel the loss of the direct form of government which Stormont provided. I am also convinced that the new Secretary of State and his colleagues will be extremely hard pushed to find ways in which the system of administration which they have taken over could be improved in efficiency or fairness. There has been an all too ready acceptance in Great Britain of the notion that since things had 'gone wrong' in Northern Ireland something must be wrong with the parliamentary and government structure. What people on this side of the Irish Sea must face up to—and that includes the British Government—is that things have gone wrong in Northern Ireland because certain people—a small but virulent section of the population—have passionately wanted things to go wrong and have worked unflaggingly towards that goal. That is an unpleasant fact, but unpleasant facts that are not squarely faced simply do not go away—if anything they loom larger and larger.

Any attempt by the British Government to de-escalate the terrorist campaign simply by means of appeasement, by turning a blind eye or by acquiescent 'containment' will be doomed to failure, and Northern Ireland, which has already suffered so much, will have an even greater burden of suffering to bear.

I opposed Mr Heath's actions, because I thought they were wrong, both morally and politically, but now that he has taken this action he must back it up in the most determined manner possible in the suppression of terrorism. Otherwise his actions will be an unmitigated disaster both for him and for us. He and his colleagues should recall very recent history and see the bitter fruits which are harvested whenever a British Government refuses to face unpleasant facts about the Ulster situation. For while the tragic path of the last few years is difficult to plot in detail, as so much is happening on so many different fronts, there is, in my opinion, one point which can be clearly defined at which a difficult position became, unnecessarily, a dangerous one. That point was the decision taken by the Labour Government, who had control of the army, not to sweep aside the barricades in 1969. Against the advice of the Northern Ireland Government Mr Wilson and his colleagues refused to face the fact that this inaction would allow the IRA to intrench themselves behind the barricades and would deliver whole areas to their thraldom.

The Labour Government instead preferred the cosier myth that a 'softly, softly' policy would allow responsible members of the minority to exercise a positive influence. History already knows who was right. It is worth recalling that when we first warned of an IRA threat, this was dismissed as Unionist hysteria. It was behind the barricades that the IRA built up their extensive command structure. The harsh facts of the situation were not faced. On the other hand, I would submit that we in the Northern Ireland Government did face facts, did face up to the challenge facing us, and did honestly and conscientiously meet our commitments. Despite the propaganda which poured out against us, we never believed in the possibility of a purely 'military' victory.

We fully recognised that if we were ever to achieve a peaceful community in Northern Ireland we would have to satisfy every citizen that his citizenship was first class, with complete justice and complete equality in every sphere and that we would have to amend our parliamentary structures and reconcile conflicting political aspirations in such a way as to enable all but the extremists to identify fully with the Northern Ireland community.

Our critics were listened to when they blackened us as reluctant reformers and accused us of feet dragging. Yet we can point to a record of constructive change which spans almost every aspect of life in Northern Ireland and which in detail not only meets but goes further than our pledges and commitments. And let no one forget that the Unionist Government was at the conference table as early as the middle of last year willing to discuss with all interested Parties ways in which the community could be brought closer together by means of structural change. Let me make it clear that that remains the position now that we are out of office—any Parties who wish to talk to us about the future are very welcome to do so. This is an important point, for I believe that, ultimately, solutions to our problems in Northern Ireland can only really be achieved by agreement between the people of Ulster themselves.

Not only did we in the Unionist Government push ahead with this work in the face of grave and growing difficulties in terms of the security situation, but we provided firm leadership for the vast majority of the population who looked to us as their representatives. Despite unbelievable provocation and suffering, our supporters have refrained from retaliatory action and from vying with our political opponents in irresponsibility. In the long run, despite the fact that our stewardship could not be faulted in any way, the Northern Ireland Government was sacrificed in the face of pressures from other sources on Mr Heath and his administration. He and his colleagues rationalised the position by saying that they could no longer tolerate a divided security responsibility. Frankly, that argument does not stand up. There was never a single incident in which the Army took an action which was not dictated by anything other than military requirements. And, in any case, would it make sense to have the long term structure of normal law and order founded upon the security arrangements of an emergency situation?

The British Government closed their eyes to an available option, namely the division of national security from normal policing and the administration of the courts. And no one should be under any illusions—they did so, not out of strength, but out of weakness. It seems to me that Mr Heath has a very poor opinion indeed of the British public's moral fibre if he does not believe that they would support firm action against the terrorists—action backed up by justice and fair dealing.

I question very much, for example, whether he has the support of British public opinion in condoning the recent scandal of allowing the gunmen in Londonderry to erect and maintain a permanent look-out tower in their area. I sincerely hope that this scandal is not symptomatic of a new 'softly, softly' policy which will take us all further down the spiral of violence and terror.

The new Secretary of State and his Ministers will, for the first time, now be dealing directly with the whole Northern Ireland situation. They will learn some hard lessons during the next twelve months and I feel sure that their view of the situation will have changed, in some important respects, by the end of the year. I will be surprised if their understanding of our position has not improved considerably in that time. In times of crisis political parties, like people, find that the inessentials fall away and they are faced with the hard facts of their existence.

The Unionist Party exists fundamentally, as its name implies, to maintain the union between Northern Ireland and the rest of the United Kingdom. It is the fear that that union is endangered by the suspension of Stormont which brought 100,000 people there to protest. During the past twelve months 247 people have died in Ulster, 2,332 have been injured. Yet there have been no reprisals, and the determination of the majority to remain British is stronger than at any time for fifty years. The majority were convinced that terror could not win. Now that confidence is shattered.

To everyone in Northern Ireland Mr Heath's initiatives are seen as a victory for terrorist's tactics, and therefore for Republicanism. Mr Hume who has demanded a 'united Ireland or nothing' now calls for the cessation of the IRA campaign because, he says, the British Government has already conceded three and a half of the four demands of his Party: the cessation of Stormont, the removal of law and order powers, the establishment of a Commission, and the review of internment—now under way. Against such a background, is it surprising that, to the people I lead, the reassurances of Mr Heath and his colleagues that we shall not be coerced into an Irish Republic have a hollow ring?

It must be the first task of the Secretary of State to reassure two-thirds of the Ulster people that their fears are unfounded. To do that now, words will not be enough. He will be judged by his actions. And what is the Unionist position? Some have suggested that it is inconsistent for my colleagues and myself to have declared on the one hand that we will not oppose Mr Whitelaw and his colleagues, and on the other that we and our supporters will steer clear of any proposed Advisory Commission. But there is all the difference in the world between advising HM Ministers—who are the elected representatives of the British nation, of which we form part—and recognising an arbitrarily-appointed Commission which would, in effect, push out even further from influence and responsibility the elected members of the temporarily suspended Northern Ireland Parliament.

My colleagues and I will always be ready to offer our advice to the Secretary of State and, in particular, we will be urging on him the priorities of the situation as we see them. We are the elected representatives of the Northern Ireland electorate; we have a right to speak out to Mr Whitelaw on behalf of those we represent; and we have every right to criticise his policies whenever we think criticism or warnings are necessary.

The basis of Unionism is an insistence that the citizens of Northern Ireland must enjoy the full benefits and full citizenship of the United Kingdom. In our opinion this can best be achieved by having our present constitutional link with Westminster, coupled with a devolved regional government of a sound, comprehensive nature. We are already ourselves in the process of making changes at

167

Stormont, but the Stormont of the future must be a worthwhile Parliament and Government and that is what we shall be campaigning for in the months ahead.

We would have nothing to do with a sham Stormont. If the British Government were to set its face against a worthwhile Stormont then I believe that Unionists will settle for nothing less than full integration with the rest of the United Kingdom, on the Scottish pattern, giving us adequate democratic representation at Westminster, full British standards and total equality with our fellow citizens in Great Britain.

We shall campaign constructively and responsibly—we have a good case. But no-one should be in any doubt that the only alternatives are those which I have described.

Nothing else will do. Nothing else could work. Nothing else could be imposed.

This is the most important fact of all to be faced by the British Government and by everyone else.

27 January 1974: 'Voices from the past are betraying our interests' an article on the future of Northern Ireland, *Sunday News*, Belfast

There has always been a British and an Irish dimension to Ulster's situation. Now, in the latter half of the 20th century we are becoming increasingly conscious of a European dimension and, indeed, a world dimension as well.

Our attitudes to our problems must, therefore, take into account not only our own immediate preferences or inclinations, but also their likely effect on British public opinion and on the status and reputation of Ulster throughout the democratic world. When we fail to bear these extra dimensions in mind, or turn inwards on ourselves assuming that all hands are against us and seek only to build walls from behind which to shout defiance, then we do a grave disservice to the cause we claim to espouse and seriously embarrass our many friends throughout the world.

We must be careful not to confuse self reliance with provincialism, nor honour with an unwillingness to admit to past mistakes.

VALUE

I firmly believe that the Union has been and should continue to be of great value to Ulster. Its economic value is a very important factor. But there are other ways in which our British citizenship is important to us; we are not simply loyal to our pockets. We believe in the Union of England, Scotland, Wales and Northern Ireland as an expression of common traditions, common interests and common loyalty to the Crown. We believe in it as a means of obtaining for the four partners together an important place in the councils of the world which none of them could secure on their own.

It is true that the relationship between Ulster and the other partners has not, in recent years, been an entirely harmonious one. Some people feel bitter and let down by those from whom they expected support and friendship. In some quarters a form of Ulster nationalism has grown up and certain politicians have expressed antagonism towards the rest of the United Kingdom.

It is temptingly easy to blame all our problems on the mistakes of others. But it would be foolish and wrong to do so. British Governments have made serious mistakes in their dealings with Ulster in the past. Of that there can be little doubt. But we need to ask ourselves why such a gap of communication opened up between the people of Ulster and the people of Great Britain, why we each failed to appreciate adequately the perspective of the other. Perhaps we had come to take the Union too much for granted and to rely too much on the glories of the past to provide security for the future. Perhaps we had just become too obsessed with our own affairs and failed to notice the reaction of disgust and horror in Great Britain at the activities of a certain section of our religious and political leaders throughout the late 1960's.

But looking back at the publicity attending these activities it is easy to see how before 1968 we in Ulster had come to be regarded by some as a rather backward cleric-ridden community of loyalist hill-billys left over from a bygone colonial age. I believe that such misapprehensions had already seriously damaged our support in Great Britain and made it easier for the Civil Rights campaign to arouse public opinion against us, and therefore those who were before 1968 indulging in a policy of street confrontations and denigration of the forces to law and order bear a heavy responsibility for what followed.

However, the Union is bigger than any one government or temporary aberrations in its policy. It would be foolish to pass a harsh judgement on its value on a short term basis. The Union is the foundation of our whole political approach: it is a concrete political expression of the fact that for us being 'British' as distinct from being Irish, English, Scottish, or Welsh only, has a meaning and a value. It brings us benefits and imposes on us duties. If it has any meaning for us we must be prepared to work to preserve it. But it also gives us a right to participate fully in the political affairs of the United Kingdom, a right which, I hope, will soon be adequately recognised by the provision of fair representation for Northern Ireland in the Commons, as recommended in the Kilbrandon Report.

INSULTS

It is in this spirit that we as a real Unionist Party have approached the proposals for a new system of government in Northern Ireland. We have not tried, nor do we intend to try to profit politically from misunderstandings between ourselves and the rest of the United Kingdom, nor to participate in the hurling of insults across the Irish Sea. Such activities only serve to weaken the Union and undermine our interests.

We do not regard the new system as perfect; the system set up by the 1920 Act also had its imperfections. But having put considerable efforts into producing policy documents and having gone to Darlington and other series of discussions to argue our case strongly we decided to give the new system a chance to operate. If it failed because of inherent defects then we believe we would have failed honourably and could expect more support for our arguments in the working out of a new solution. If we succeeded in spite of the vast difficulties we believed that Ulstermen would deserve and would receive much credit for sinking long standing and serious differences in the common cause of peace and economic progress.

BITTER

The alternative—to harp back continually to 'the good old days' when all was well and to insist that turning the clock back will solve all our ills—is to lead people on a course which can result only in futility, frustration and bitterness. Whatever the rights and wrongs of 1968, we are now in 1974 with a new system of government backed virtually unanimously by the Conservative, Labour and Liberal parties at Westminster and providing safeguards for our fundamental principles. In a situation where Ulster has already suffered from a lack of adequate democratic government for 21 months what is needed now is a positive and dynamic approach to mould and use the new institutions into effective instruments of government for the good of all our people.

Coalitions are a very common form of government in the democratic world and seldom entail a loss of party identity by the parties involved. The Constitution Act lays down certain parameters for an Executive, in effect that there must be substantial support for it in both the Protestant and Catholic communities. But within that flexible parameter there is scope for various forms of coalition. The present Executive is a freely entered coalition of those parties prepared to work within the framework of the Constitution Act and opposed by those Assemblymen not prepared to do so. None of the parties were under any compulsion to take up the attitudes which they did. Those not in the Executive are, therefore, self-excluded.

MERITS

While the Executive can agree on common policies and command a majority in the Assembly it will remain in Office. When it can no longer do so a new coalition will have to be formed. That is not an unreasonable way of governing a country, and I believe people are beginning to see the merits of power sharing.

The Sunningdale Agreement as explained and denounced by various politicians bears little relationship to the document I helped to negotiate at Sunningdale. It is hard to think of anything else about which more myths, half truths and untruths have been assiduously pedalled by politicians seeking to whip up and exploit the very real and understandable fears of many Unionists. It is a measure of the distortion that has occurred that one needs to begin by saying what the Council of Ireland is not.

It is not a half way house to a United Ireland. Indeed, it underlines partition in a way never previously done. It was through fear of doing this that the Dublin Government refused to nominate representatives to the Council of Ireland set up under the 1920 Act.

CONSENT

It does not infringe on the sovereignty of the United Kingdom or give the Republic any jurisdiction over Northern Ireland. It is an intergovernmental agency of an unexceptional kind depending on the unanimous agreement of all its members and the approval of the Dail and Northern Ireland Assembly for all its activities. A supranational agency is one which can take decisions without the consent of one of its members. This the Council of Ireland clearly cannot do.

It does not make political intervention in the affairs of Northern Ireland by the Republic more likely. The Republic has always attempted to interfere, usually through the London Government. Now it will be dealing directly with the people of the North themselves on a basis of mutual recognition and respect and the people of the North will, for the first time, have an international platform from which to state their case. It is an opportunity for positive rather than defensive politics, and I have great confidence in the ability of all Ulstermen to make use of this opportunity effectively.

Sunningdale is a recognition of the conflicting political aspirations in Ireland and their right to democratic expression. It also provides a great opportunity to secure the defeat of terrorism. Time will show that these are gains worth having.

VARIETY

What are the alternative policies which we have been offered? There has been sufficient variety to stock a political supermarket— negotiated independence, total integration, a return to the Stormont system, a federal Ireland, a nine-county Ulster, etc. But the ease and rapidity with which the various political salesmen have changed their favourite packaged solutions has led to a great deal of confusion.

In March 1972, Ian Paisley was arguing for total integration and a suspension of Stormont.

In August 1972, John Taylor advocated negotiated independence as the only alternative to the old Stormont system.

In March 1973, William Craig supported the same view. But in October 1973, the VUPP, DUP, and "unpledged" Unionist Assemblymen all met and agreed to declare their joint support for total integration as the only viable alternative. But since then we have seen Mr Baird, a leading VUPP member write to an English paper advocating negotiated independence, and in December, Captain Ardill wrote a lengthy letter to the Belfast News Letter attempting to advocate the benefits of independence. Now we see Mr Paisley, too, casting around for a means of abandoning his policy of integration.

It is hardly surprising, in view of such complete indecision and total lack of any real policy, that the people of Ulster are confused. It is in the interests of those who lack any policy to keep people confused and to attack others in the hope that their own inadequacies may go unnoticed. But people are beginning to see through all the political kite flying carefully designed to test the air for any new breeze which might provide a little power.

The activities of these side line experts has been a betrayal of the interests of Ulster. At each negotiating hurdle since Darlington they have sniped at and weakened and attempted to undermine the Unionist negotiators and yet they have the impertinence to criticise the agreements negotiated. They are a completely negative force. As peace and stability grow the consistent and constructive approach of the Unionist Party will be increasingly recognised and the tide of events will pass by these voices from the past and consign to them the oblivion which they deserve.

It is now generally accepted that neither independence nor integration are viable policies. In the search for a new solution Mr Boal's ideas for a Federal Ireland appear: A Protestant state and a United Ireland outside the United Kingdom all at once. You can have your cake and eat it Mr Boal assures us! What an extremist's paradise!

FALSE

But Mr Boal conveniently omits to mention some very basic and rather embarrassing points. His scheme would involve a fundamental change of allegiance to Dublin; we would all have Irish passports; our flag would be the tricolour—perhaps with a 'Red Hand' in the centre; we would have an all-Ireland army and navy; our foreign policy would be determined by Dublin and we would be outside NATO. But most important of all, Mr Boal does not say what is to happen to the Roman Catholics in Northern Ireland. He is only interested in 'the Protestant way of life' he says, though he fails to tell us what particular life-style that phrase encompasses. And of course the solution is based on false assumptions: that the Council of Ireland is a back door way to a United Ireland and that the Union is not worth preserving. Unionists reject both these propositions. In the 1970's the old slogans of 1912 and the old methods are just not good enough. All the people of these islands face a common future. Our economic, social, and political destinies are tied up together in a world where the mass media, vast travel and modern methods of communication are leading to a drawing together of the neighbouring states.

In the context of the EEC I foresee the Republic of Ireland returning to a closer relationship with the United Kingdom. Indeed, that process has already begun; the old isolationist, anti-British and Catholic nationalist sentiments of the De Valera age are slowly but surely dying out. Would it not be tragic if at this stage in history it was Ulster which was to turn away from her partners in the United Kingdom, bitter and introverted and with few friends throughout the democratic world.

The Ulster I intend to work for is a peaceful one which it will be a pleasure to live in, an Ulster whose inhabitants will be proud to declare their allegiance wherever they may travel, and an Ulster which will have won respect throughout the world for the way in which its people have united to overcome years of violence and political disappointments which would have soured a lesser people. That is the Ulster which I now believe is within our grasp.

APPENDIX 3

Executive Policy

January 1974: Economic and social aims, a statement by the Northern Ireland Executive

GENERAL OBJECTIVES

1 The formation of a multi-Party Executive requires, inter alia, prior agreement on a social and economic programme to be implemented whilst in office.

We are agreed that the basic objectives of such a programme should be to achieve rising standards of living, sustained full employment and the greatest possible measure of equality of opportunity and social and economic justice.

We are also agreed that the first step towards achieving these is for the Executive to establish a comprehensive social and economic plan for Northern Ireland, backed by a central planning unit, which, in the light of detailed analysis of the full range of economic and social problems facing the community, will establish clear-cut and realistic economic and social goals.

The plan will also determine the detailed policies and public expenditure programmes needed to achieve these agreed objectives over the years to come. It will include clear-cut targets in the fields of income per head and employment levels, which will be designed to achieve at least parity in real terms with Great Britain, and the consequent investment programmes for infrastructure, social investment including housing, education and training, and State and private industry.

We appreciate that the preparation and execution of such programmes will involve the full measure of freedom of decision which Westminster agreed to devolve to the new Executive. We also realise that the achievement of our basic objectives may require us to discuss with Westminster the necessity for some further Executive responsibility over taxation in Northern Ireland.

2 The following sections elaborate the statements contained in

175

the preceding paragraph and describe in general terms a number of the measures which, we are agreed, seem likely to appear in any comprehensive Social and Economic Programme for Northern Ireland.

GENERAL ECONOMIC POLICY

3 In order to achieve our basic economic objectives it will be necessary to examine various problems that underlie overall unemployment figures in order to produce a more effective reduction of unemployment.

Our clear priority is to provide full employment for the people of Northern Ireland. Enterprise Ulster in the short-term must be given a new and strengthened role having regard to the employment position in particular areas.

It will also be important to seek methods of increasing Northern Ireland participation and influence in EEC. In particular we are determined to obtain the maximum use of EEC monies for local regional development.

GENERAL REGIONAL PHYSICAL STRATEGY

4 We agree that it will be important to develop the policy of Growth and Key Centres, both for industrial promotion and for economy in services. Secondly, in our physical planning policy, the tradition and character of each locality must be respected and its true potential developed.

INDUSTRIAL DEVELOPMENT

5 Our aim will be to obtain the maximum employment opportunities throughout Northern Ireland. Existing machinery will be maintained and extended and new machinery developed to facilitate Government involvement in promising industrial enterprises and ventures, which offer the prospect of new and expanding employment opportunities.

We will also aim to ensure that Northern Ireland remains a most attractive base for new and existing industries by virtue of wide, generous and flexible industrial incentives, comprehensive industrial training and good industrial relations. The range of incentives offered will be reviewed to ensure that they are as competitive and selective as possible.

The present momentum of the Local Enterprise Development Unit will be maintained and reinforced.

ENERGY

6   A review of energy needs and resources will be undertaken with special reference to mineral development both on and off-shore.

HOUSING

7   In order to tackle the housing problem effectively and eradicate the serious lack of basic facilities and services in many areas we need:

a   a housing target of 20,000 houses per year once the productivity of the construction industry has been increased;

b   speedier re-development and a bigger housing conversion and improvement programme;

c   measures to render the construction industry more streamlined and efficient and train more skilled operatives;

d   to examine measures with a view to control of urban land speculation and prices;

e   to develop water and sewerage services to meet identified needs;

f   to encourage development of voluntary housing agencies such as Housing Associations and co-operatives;

g   to encourage greater tenant involvement in planning, management and maintenance of housing estates;

h   to continue wherever necessary the present policy of public acquisition of houses in the private rented sector;

i   measures to encourage home ownership in every way possible;

j   measures to ensure that the private sector can make its full contribution to the housing programme;

k   to promote the growth of integrated housing; and

l   to pay greater attention than in the past to the environmental quality of housing estates, public and private.

These proposals will involve a radical re-examination of the whole system of housing finance in Northern Ireland.

COMMUNITY RELATIONS

8   It should be made clear at the outset that every aspect of the Northern Ireland problem involves community relations. All members of the Executive will be actively concerned to improve community relations.

A reappraisal of the existing institutional arrangements in this field will be a priority task.

AGRICULTURE

9   Agriculture is of paramount importance to Northern Ireland. Whilst recognising the role of the EEC in the formulation of

agricultural policy, we agree that the Executive must strive to take all necessary steps to increase the prosperity of Northern Ireland's agriculture.

In particular, we believe we must make full use of grass, our major natural asset. The intensive livestock industry must also be assisted to surmount the major problems which it is facing from the rising costs of imported feeding stuffs. The Executive will also take steps to improve the viability of small farms, including those in horticulture.

If agriculture in Northern Ireland is to contribute to the achievement of our overall social and economic objectives, it will be necessary to devise programmes to encourage co-operative farming, food processing and timber-based industries. A thorough investigation of our fishing potential will be set in hand and steps will also be taken to encourage fish processing and boat building.

TRANSPORT

10 There is need for a detailed re-examination of the entire transport system including the administration of harbours and a detailed review of the role of the Northern Ireland Transport Holding Company. As part of the policy of more balanced development there should be development of port and airport facilities in the North West.

Using the latest techniques, we shall also wish to study the interplay of public and private transport and to assess the social and economic value as well as the financial costs of roads, buses, railways and car parking.

We are also agreed upon the need to open discussions with Westminster on our powers in relation to shipping and air services—both freight and passenger—which are crucial to the future development of the economy of Northern Ireland.

CONSERVATION AND THE ENVIRONMENT

11 There is a need for encouragement and re-inforcement of the new arrangements in Northern Ireland relating to conservation in order to marshal all the necessary resources and to harmonise management policies and legislation.

TOURISM

12 We are agreed on the need to explore the possibilities of providing facilities in advance of need in order to pioneer markets for the future.

EDUCATION

13 The ideal of equal educational opportunity for all and the primacy of parental rights are the principles on which our educational system should be based. In the present context the following changes will be required:

a the introduction of a policy of universal nursery education;

b the radical re-examination of the present selection procedures for secondary education and the consequent re-organisation of secondary education;

c recognition of educational priority areas based on social need;

d the creation of machinery in the field of higher education so that our considerable resources can be co-ordinated in the best interests of the community as a whole; and

e a detailed investigation of the role of education in the promotion of community harmony and the development of pilot experiments, after consultation with interested parties, in integrated education.

CULTURE AND COMMUNICATIONS

14 We understand the need for sensitivity and care in these fields but believe that every effort should be made to promote further understanding of the variety of our culture and traditions.

PRICES AND INCOMES

15 This is largely the responsibility of Westminster but the Northern Ireland Executive should co-ordinate Government agencies here and create adequate price policing methods as well as giving positive encouragement to the development of voluntary consumer associations.

INDUSTRIAL DEMOCRACY

16 Studies and research leading to legislation to develop the concept of greater worker participation in the management of industry should be set in train.

ELIMINATION OF POVERTY

17 Research into the extent of poverty, the extent of disability, the extent of unmet need for community welfare services in Northern Ireland and the evaluation of services received will be a priority task for the Executive, with a view to reforming such parts of the system of social services as are necessary adequately to fulfil the objective of eradicating poverty.

Without prejudice to the principle of parity with Great Britain, consideration should be given to the creation of Northern Ireland as a pilot area for reforms in the field of family allowances, supplementary benefits, and the rationalisation of means-tested benefits with a view to using the resources of the social services to make the most effective possible attack on poverty.

Among our first priorities will be the elimination of poverty and the rehabilitation of all those—especially the young—adversely affected by the recent violence.

December 1973: Tripartite agreement on the Council of Ireland, the communique issued following the Sunningdale Conference

1   The Conference between the British and Irish Governments and the Parties involved in the Northern Ireland Executive (Designate) met at Sunningdale on 6, 7, 8 and 9 December, 1973.

2   During the Conference, each delegation stated their position on the status of Northern Ireland.

3   The Taoiseach said that the basic principle of the conference was that the participants had tried to see what measure of agreement of benefit to all the people concerned could be secured. In doing so, all had reached accommodation with one another on practical arrangements. But none had compromised and none had asked others to compromise, in relation to basic aspirations. The people of the Republic, together with a minority in Northern Ireland as represented by the SDLP delegation, continued to uphold the aspiration towards a united Ireland. The only unity they wanted to see was a unity established by consent.

4   Mr Brian Faulkner said that delegates from Northern Ireland came to the conference as representatives of apparently incompatible sets of political aspirations who had found it possible to reach agreement to join together in Government because each accepted that in doing so they were not sacrificing principles or aspirations. The desire of the majority of the people of Northern Ireland to remain part of the United Kingdom, as represented by the Unionist and Alliance delegations, remained firm.

5   The Irish Government fully accepted and solemnly declared that there could be no change in the status of Northern Ireland until a majority of the people of Northern Ireland desired a change in that status.

The British Government solemnly declared that it was, and would remain, their policy to support the wishes of the majority of the people of Northern Ireland. The present status of Northern Ireland is that it is part of the United Kingdom. If in the future the majority of the people of Northern Ireland should indicate a wish to become part of a united Ireland, the British Government would support that wish.

6 The conference agreed that a formal agreement incorporating the declarations of the British and Irish Governments would be signed at the formal stage of the conference and registered at the United Nations.

7 The conference agreed that a Council of Ireland would be set up. It would be confined to representatives of the two parts of Ireland, with appropriate safeguards for the British Government's financial and other interests. It would comprise a Council of Ministers with executive and harmonising functions and a consultative role, and a Consultative Assembly with advisory and review functions. The Council of Ministers would act by unanimity and would comprise a core of seven members of the Irish Government and an equal number of members of the Northern Ireland Executive with provision for the participation of other non-voting members of the Irish Government and the Northern Ireland Executive or administration when matters within their Departmental competence were discussed.

The Council of Ministers would control the functions of the Council. The Chairmanship would rotate on an agreed basis between representatives of the Irish Government and of the Northern Ireland Executive. Arrangements would be made for the location of the first meeting and the location of subsequent meetings would be determined by the Council of Ministers. The Consultative Assembly would consist of 60 members, 30 members from Dail Eireann chosen by the Dail on the basis of Proportional Representation by the single transferable vote, and 30 members from the Northern Ireland Assembly chosen by that Assembly and also on that basis. The members of the Consultative Assembly would be paid allowances. There would be a Secretariat to the Council, which would be kept as small as might be commensurate with efficiency in the operation of the Council.

The Secretariat would service the institutions of the Council and would, under the Council of Ministers, supervise the carrying out of the executive and harmonising functions and the consultative role of the Council. The Secretariat would be headed by a Secretary-General.

Following the appointment of a Northern Ireland Executive, the Irish Government and the Northern Ireland Executive would nominate their representatives to a Council of Ministers. The Council of Ministers would then appoint a Secretary-General and decide upon the location of its permanent headquarters. The Secretary-General would be directed to proceed with the drawing up of plans for such headquarters. The Council of Ministers would also make arrangements for the recruitment of the staff of the Secretariat in a manner and on conditions which would, as far as is practicable, be consistent with those applying to public servants in the two administrations.

8   In the context of its harmonising functions and consultative role, the Council of Ireland would undertake important work relating, for instance, to the impact of EEC membership. As for Executive functions, the first step would be to define and agree these in detail. The conference therefore decided that, in view of the administrative complexities involved, studies would at once be set in hand to identify and, prior to the formal stage of the conference, report on areas of common interest in relation to which a Council of Ireland would take executive decisions, and, in appropriate cases, be responsible for carrying those decisions into effect. In carrying out these studies, and also in determining what should be done by the Council in terms of harmonisation, the objectives to be borne in mind would include the following:

1   To achieve the best utilisation of scarce skills, expertise and resources;

2   To avoid, in the interests of economy and efficiency, unnecessary duplication of effort; and

3   To ensure complementary rather than competitive effort where this is to the advantage of agriculture, commerce and industry.

In particular, these studies would be directed to identifying, for the purposes of Executive action by the Council of Ireland, suitable aspects of activities in the following broad fields:

A   Exploitation, conservation and development of natural resources and the environment;

B   Agricultural matters (including Agricultural Research, Animal Health and operational aspects of the common Agriculture Policy), Forestry and Fisheries;

C   Co-operative ventures in the fields of trade and industry;

D Electricity Generation;
E Tourism;
F Roads and Transport;
G Advisory Services in the field of Public Health;
H Sport, Culture and the Arts.

It would be for the Oireachtas and the Northern Ireland Assembly to legislate from time to time as to the extent of functions to be devolved to the Council of Ireland. Where necessary, the British Government will co-operate in this devolution of functions. Initially, the functions to be vested would be those identified in accordance with the procedures set out above and decided, at the formal stage of the conference, to be transferred.

9 i During the initial period following the establishment of the Council, the revenue of the Council would be provided by means of grants from the two administrations in Ireland towards agreed projects and budgets, according to the nature of the service involved.

ii It was also agreed that further studies would be put in hand forthwith and completed as soon as possible of methods of financing the Council after the initial period which would be consonant with the responsibilities and functions assigned to it.

iii It was agreed that the cost of the Secretariat of the Council of Ireland would be shared equally, and other services would be financed broadly in proportion to where expenditure or benefit accrues.

iv The amount of money required to finance the Council's activities will depend upon the functions assigned to it from time to time.

v While Britain continues to pay subsidies to Northern Ireland, such payments would not involve Britain participating in the Council, it being accepted nevertheless that it would be legitimate for Britain to safeguard in an appropriate way her financial involvement in Northern Ireland.

10 It was agreed by all parties that persons committing crimes of violence, however motivated, in any part of Ireland should be brought to trial irrespective of the part of Ireland in which they are located. The concern which large sections of the people of Northern Ireland felt about this problem was in particular forcefully expressed by the representatives of the Unionist and Alliance Parties.

The representatives of the Irish Government stated that they understood and fully shared this concern. Different ways of solving this problem were discussed; among them were the amendment of legislation operating in the two jurisdictions on extradition, the creation of a common law enforcement area in which an All-Ireland Court would have jurisdiction, and the extension of the jurisdiction of domestic courts so as to enable them to try offences committed outside the jurisdiction. It was agreed that problems of considerable legal complexity were involved and that the British and Irish Governments would jointly set up a commission to consider all the proposals put forward at the Conference and to recommend as a matter of extreme urgency the most effective means of dealing with those who commit these crimes. The Irish Government undertook to take immediate and effective legal steps so that persons coming within their jurisdiction and accused of murder, however motivated, committed in Northern Ireland will be brought to trial, and it was agreed that any similar reciprocal action that may be needed in Northern Ireland be taken by the appropriate authorities.

11   It was agreed that the Council would be invited to consider in what way the principles of the European Convention on Human Rights and Fundamental Freedoms would be exercised in domestic legislation in each part of Ireland. It would recommend whether further legislation or the creation of other institutions, administrative or judicial, is required in either part or embracing the whole island to provide additional protection in the field of human rights. Such recommendations could include the functions of an ombudsman or commissioner for complaints, or other arrangements of a similar nature which the Council of Ireland might think appropriate.

12   The Conference also discussed the question of policing and the need to ensure public support for and identification with the police service throughout the whole community. It was agreed that no single set of proposals would achieve these aims overnight, and that time would be necessary. The Conference expressed the hope that the wide range of agreement that had been reached, and the consequent formation of a power-sharing Executive, would make a major contribution to the creation of an atmosphere throughout the community where there would be widespread support for an identification with all the institutions of Northern Ireland.

13   It was broadly accepted that the two parts of Ireland are to a considerable extent inter-dependent in the whole field of law and order, and that the problems of political violence and identification with the Police Service cannot be solved without taking account of that fact.

14 Accordingly, the British Government stated that, as soon as the security problems were resolved and the new institutions were seen to be working effectively, they would wish to discuss the devolution of responsibility for normal policing and how this might be achieved with the Northern Ireland Executive and the Police.

15 With a view to improving policing throughout the island and developing community identification with and support for the Police Services, the Governments concerned will co-operate under the auspices of a Council of Ireland through their respective Police Authorities. To this end, the Irish Government would set up a Police Authority, appointments to which would be made after consultation with the Council of Ministers of the Council of Ireland. In the case of the Northern Ireland Police Authority, appointments would be made after consultation with the Northern Ireland Executive, which would consult with the Council of Ministers of the Council of Ireland. When the two Police Authorities are constituted, they will make their own arrangements to achieve the objectives set out above.

16 An independent complaints procedure for dealing with complaints against the Police will be set up.

17 The Secretary of State for Northern Ireland will set up an all-party Committee from the Assembly to examine how best to introduce effective policing throughout Northern Ireland with particular reference to the need to achieve public identification with the Police.

18 The Conference took note of a reaffirmation by the British Government of their firm commitment to bring detention to an end in Northern Ireland for all sections of the community as soon as the security situation permits, and noted also that the Secretary of State for Northern Ireland hopes to be able to bring into use his Statutory Powers of selective release in time for a number of detainees to be released before Christmas.

19 The British Government stated that, in the light of the decisions reached at the Conference, they would now seek the authority of Parliament to devolve full powers to the Northern Ireland Executive and Northern Ireland Assembly as soon as possible. The formal appointment of the Northern Ireland Executive would then be made.

20 The Conference agreed that a formal conference would be held early in the New Year at which the British and Irish Governments and the Northern Ireland Executive would meet together to

consider reports on the studies which have been commissioned and to sign the agreement reached.

24 January 1974: First policy speech in the Northern Ireland Assembly as Chief Executive

Our first decision as an Executive was to table a Motion of Confidence here. We want to establish, right from the start, to whom it is that we are responsible. There are those who say, and will no doubt say again, that we are an undemocratic Executive. Let us put that matter to the test, and without delay. We are responsible not to the Secretary of State—any more than our predecessors in Northern Ireland Governments were responsible to the Governor who appointed them—but to the people of Northern Ireland as represented by this Assembly. Incidentally, I think if the people of Northern Ireland saw the antics of some of the people who operated here this afternoon and on Tuesday, they would say they chose well when they made us the Executive. We have been told by some self-appointed constitutional pundits that the whole basis of government here has been changed utterly from all we knew in the past and that, in particular, this Executive has a life quite independent of the Legislature.

Mr Speaker, the Government of Ireland Act, under which Governments operated here for more than half a century, nowhere spelled out the relationship between Government and Paliament. That relationship developed out of centuries of parliamentary practice, but at its heart were some simple realities. A Government which cannot pass its legislation is a cipher. A Government which are refused a grant of Supply cannot function. A Government which are defeated in the Legislature on a crucial issue of confidence cannot survive. These were realities before; they remain realities now.

And so we accept that our responsibility is first of all to this Assembly, and that our right course is to seek at once an indication of its confidence and support. We do so on a clearly phrased and unambiguous Motion. If that Motion were not to commend itself to this Assembly, we should at once ask the Secretary of State to accept the resignation of the Administration. But there is a corollary to this. As democrats, as parliamentarians, we submit ourselves at once to this democratic test. We place our principles and our policy before the elected representatives chosen by the people of Northern Ireland only months ago. And if those principles and policy are upheld here, we believe we acquire certain rights: not the right to escape scrutiny or criticism, but the right to a fair hearing which is accorded in any democratic country to the Government of the day.

As we meet this Assembly for the first time as an Executive in being I believe that Members will expect of us three things. First, an indication of the state of the country as we find it. It is now not far short of two years since Ulstermen headed the Departments of Government here, and were in a position to report to the elected representatives of the people on the overall condition of our affairs. Second, I propose to give to this Assembly an account of our intentions as an Executive: of the principles by which we will be guided, the legislative and other steps we will ask the Assembly to support, and the methods by which we shall proceed towards our goals. And third, I am sure that Members will wish to hear from me an impression of those major political and constitutional questions which concern us all. It will be my intention to give to the Assembly a full report under each of these heads.

But before I begin I want to make one thing very clear. As this debate proceeds a number of my colleagues on the Front Bench behind me will also come to this Dispatch Box. They are men drawn, as the House knows, from different political parties. But there is not in our Executive different categories of member. We have agreed unanimously that we will operate in all our affairs according to the principle of collective responsibility. Not one of us will be coming to this Dispatch Box just to speak for himself or for his party. We are the Northern Ireland Executive. We have taken an oath together to serve the interest of Northern Ireland and its people, and that we shall do together.

What we are determined to do is to offer a lead to the people of Northern Ireland in a future where enjoyment of rights will be accompanied, as it must be, by the acceptance of obligations. Each individual must be prepared to meet his fair share of the cost of services provided for the community as a whole. In dealing with debts which have accumulated we will be concerned to prevent undue hardship; but such debts must, in fairness to others, be paid in full.

Now I turn, first of all, to the state of Northern Ireland as we assume office. One of our earliest decisions was to call in the most senior members of the Civil Service, and to hear together a detailed report on the progress of Northern Ireland and the problems which lie ahead. I wanted to see us facing all our problems together right from the start; not concentrating so much on the affairs of one department or another that we fail to see the total picture.

And so the first thing I can tell the House is that we have received into our hands an administrative machine which has to its credit a marvellous record of accomplishment in difficult times. Who could have imagined that, in spite of all the adverse circumstances, unemployment affected by the energy crisis; that the promotion of new jobs would be rising; and that Northern Ireland would in some respects be displaying more economic health and energy than almost any other part of the United Kingdom?

Three factors have contributed to this situation. First, there has been the basic determination and resilience of our community. Those who have sought to bring about despair and disintegration have failed. Second, we have had in Northern Ireland a government machine second to none, which has gone on doing its job with total loyalty and dedication through bombs, bullets, disorder, changes of government and the rest. Third—and we must recognise this—we have continued to receive quite exceptional support from the United Kingdom Government. That, it may be said, is no more than our right. Indeed it is our right, as a part of the United Kingdom.

As part of the nation we, like other parts, both contribute to the whole and derive benefits from it. But no one should be in any doubt as to the importance of these benefits for every man, woman and child in Northern Ireland. We have all had to realise lately how painful it is when the energy tap is suddenly and unexpectedly screwed down. What seemed one day a remote crisis soon began to hit everyone, in the office, shop or factory. We have had a very striking demonstration of the fact that Northern Ireland does not live and cannot live in a world of its own. We should take that lesson very much to heart.

There is another very important respect in which we rely upon others to make a major contribution to our progress, and that is in the field of industrial investment. We have built up our economic base by attracting such investment not only from the rest of the United Kingdom but in a major degree from North America and Western Europe. In that context my colleagues and I share the great concern which is felt at the disappearance of Mr Thomas Neidermayer. Here is a man who has contributed much to the welfare of Northern Ireland, both through his own firm of Grundig and through his general assistance to the whole industrial promotion campaign.

I have known Thomas Neidermayer personally for over 12 years and have a very high regard for his ability. I am sure I would be speaking for all of us in this Assembly in sending to his wife and family our earnest prayer that he may shortly be restored to them in good health and strength. [*Hon. Members: Hear, hear.*] It is nothing short of tragedy that a guest in our land, a good friend of the Ulster people and indeed a consular representative of his Government, should now be the cause of such justifiable concern. All of us hope and pray that he will yet be found safe and well, and I appeal to anyone who has the slightest scrap of information which might assist his safe return to communicate it to the police. I want also to place it on record on behalf of all of us that we appreciate profoundly all that our German industries and nationals, in the best spirit of European partnership, have already contributed to the economy and the life of Northern Ireland.

I have said that in many ways we have found our economy remarkably strong and vigorous. But of course there are serious black spots. The housing programme, faced as it is by all kinds of difficulties, has fallen away badly, and many aspects of our life continue to be poisoned by violence and the fruits of violence. Moreover, the very serious economic situation in the nation and the world casts a growing shadow across our future hopes. It is not a time to waste our substance or divert our efforts.

I turn now to our plans for the future. When the three parties which joined together to form this Executive first met we agreed that we ought to produce a statement of the broad social and economic objectives which we will pursue in office. We knew, of course, that detailed policies and programmes would have to be worked out once we were in office, and could deploy the full resources of the Government machine. But we believed that this Assembly, and the people of Northern Ireland as a whole, should know in what direction we proposed to move and so we agreed between us a comprehensive Statement of Social and Economic Aims, which we have now published.

This is not, nor was it intended to be, a fully worked-out and detailed plan for Northern Ireland's future. If an Administration, within a month of taking office, were to promulgate such a plan, it could only mean that they had adopted uncritically the proposals of others. We are not going to provide that sort of Government. Our detailed proposals, when we make them, will be the result of careful work and considered judgment. The Statement of Aims should be considered as our manifesto. We will now shape these principles into legislation and effective policy.

In the meantime I hope that Members, and indeed everyone in this community, will study the Statement of Aims very carefully. This is what we offer Northern Ireland in place of violence, in place of dissension, in place of endless and unproductive controversy. It is a statement directed to real things: to jobs and houses and schools and hospitals; to the sick, the weak, the young, the poor and the unskilled. It offers our people a real way forward. The work of turning these broad policy objectives into practical programmes for the future is now being pushed forward with the utmost sense of urgency. The Government machine is geared as never before to identifying our problems, seeking for solutions and converting these solutions into men and money, bricks and mortar. We are preparing to move ahead, in full consultation with both sides of industry.

We have behind us, in the White Paper, a commitment by the British Government to work for the elimination of the gap in standards between Northern Ireland and Great Britain. We cannot expect this to be achieved in the short term, or in every field at the same pace, and the allocation of resources to Northern Ireland will be crucial. But when this Executive discusses with the Secretary of State and with the British Government the financing of its pro-grammes it will do so in the conviction that nothing second-rate or second-class is acceptable in Northern Ireland, and we will expect steady progress towards those goals which the White Paper has set.

I will now turn to just a few of those fields upon which we will be concentrating our efforts in the months ahead. In the economic area I have always been convinced that Northern Ireland's principal resource is its manpower. Unskilled and untrained manpower is a dormant resource which cannot be tapped or harnessed, but with proper manpower planning we have one of the primary assets of any developing economy. That is why we have now created a separate Department of Manpower Services which, in close concert with both sides of industry, can concentrate all its energies upon the needs and the potential of our labour force. Our fundamental aim is the creation of a free and open society based on equality of opportunity. We want to afford all our people the opportunity to reach their full potential; to find ways of bringing far more of the jobless within the scope of the active labour market; to create conditions conducive to increased earnings while keeping our costs competitive and to foster the good industrial relations which have been so distinctive a feature in Northern Ireland. In this context my colleagues and I look forward to receiving in the next few months the report of the Review Body on Industrial Relations to which the CBI and the Northern Ireland Committee of the ICTU have been devoting so much time and attention under the auspices of the Department. Action in such fields as these is a base for further economic expansion.

Although the difficulties posed by the short-term fuel crisis and its economic repercussions are all too obvious, we cannot and will not plan on the basis of stagnation or decline. We must be ready to seize future opportunities, using any pause in economic advance as an opportunity better to equip ourselves. We can now deploy a most sophisticated range of aids to industrial investment, including in exceptional cases and in areas of special difficulty the possibility of up to 100 per cent. public financing. We are determined in this field to be an active Administration which will seek out suitable projects for the unemployment black spots. These gross disparities in our employment pattern are unacceptable in principle and must be tackled energetically by every means available to us.

In harmony with EEC and UK policies the Department of Agriculture will continue to help the agricultural industry to become more competitive through improvement of farm structure, assistance to the extensive livestock industries, emphasis on encouraging co-operation where feasible, increased output per acre—particularly from grassland—and still better marketing The emphasis on amenities and recreational facilities in forests and waterways will be maintained, as will the emphasis on expanding the fishing fleet and angling facilities.

Another new Department, the Department of the Environment, will now be responsible for the administration of a number of vital community services, some of which passed into central control from the old local authorities on 1 October last. I single out for special mention the gallant Fire Service, which has served this community so well throughout the stresses of recent years. In addition, roads, transport, water and conservation—all the services affecting the life of literally every person in this community—will be operated directly by the new Department.

The creation of a Department of Housing, Local Government and

Planning is intended to demonstrate three aims and to provide us with the machinery for achieving those aims. First, we intend to place a new emphasis on the housing responsibilities of Government, to respond to the undoubted concern of all Assemblymen for the housing conditions of their constituents, and to allocate the task clearly to one member of the Executive as his main duty. Second, we want to see to it that the head of the Department, through his local government responsibilities, is able to keep in close touch with local opinion in the one other level of elected authority—the highly important new system of district councils.

Third, we are determined to ensure that we do not allow ourselves to be mesmerised into simply building houses for their own sake but, through the planning work of the Department, to control and shape land use in all its many forms. We aim not just to construct dwellings but to provide the best possible conditions under which homes may be provided and maintained in pleasant surroundings with full-scale amenities and safe access to work, shopping, recreation and all the other requirements of the good life which we wish our people to enjoy.

We have vital objectives in the social sphere also. In the new area board structure for health and personal social services we have an effective means to plan, for the first time, really co-ordinated programmes of health and social care; to ensure that we raise progressively our standards in parity with Great Britain, but taking full account of our special needs; and to open up a new concept of comprehensive social welfare services, both by developing our statutory services and by tapping and enlarging the reservoir of voluntary effort. We want to see the problems of poverty tackled in our society—problems with multiple causes and demanding multiple remedies. It will be our aim to ensure that the social security system meets the needs of our people as fully and humanely as possible, and that the social security agencies work in the closest collaboration with social welfare and other agencies which have a major part to play in the relief of distress and of the many complex social problems associated with deprivation.

At this point I leave the script and mention an individual, which I am sure I ought not to do in debate. I have to say, however, that in my view the man who heads the Department of Health and Social Services has a very great and very sincere concern for this type of work. [Hon. Members: *Hear, hear.*]

In the field of education we have seen steady progress in what is and will, no doubt, continue to be a developing service. In 1973 reports on the important subjects of the organisation of secondary education and the in-service training of teachers were published. We are also actively considering the development of nursery education, further improvements in the pupil-teacher ratio and how best to meet the increased demands for adult and further education. I know that there will be continuing discussion of the relationships between our controlled and voluntary schools and the structure of our education system in an effort to build and develop co-operation between all sections of that system in the interests of our young people. These are but some of the issues to which my colleague who heads the Department of Education will be turning his attention in this debate and in the coming months.

The Department of Community Relations is being developed and strengthened. I would mention today two such developments in particular. First, the Department is assuming responsibility for sport and recreation throughout Northern Ireland. Second, it is strengthening its own team of departmental representatives on the ground, both in urban and rural areas. A most important part of their job will be to see that the Government machine is alerted to acute local problems and that misunderstandings do not arise through any lack of communication.

I have not been able to do more than give a very broad, general survey of the activities which will be going forward in the Departments. In many of these fields new legislation will be required. The Executive cannot, at this stage, give the kind of formal statement of its detailed legislative intentions which was the first business of each Session of the Northern Ireland Parliament. There are two reasons for this. Although Departments have, of course, been carrying forward their work throughout direct rule, we now need time to convert our own policy aims into detailed legislative proposals. Secondly, we must take account of those provisions of the Constitution Act which enjoin us to consult committees of the Assembly as we develop new policy. Because of these constraints we can give only a general impression at this stage, and what we say is, of course, subject to the views expressed in Consultative Committees, to which the Executive will at all times pay the closest attention.

In the special circumstances which apply as the new system comes into operation there will be certain legislation which cannot be considered in Consultative Committees, for practical reasons of urgency. In particular, there is an urgent need, before the end of the current financial year, for technical financial legislation: a Consolidated Fund Measure, following on Supplementary Estimates and a Vote on Account and a Measure to increase certain existing statutory limits on expenditure. We shall require a Measure for the appropriation of Main Estimates and an Order to determine the regional rate. We shall also be considering how best to replace the traditional Budget Statement, as, for example, by a White Paper which would set out information about public expenditure and receipts.

Another particularly urgent piece of legislation will be a Measure to extend assistance to electricity and gas undertakings to enable them to offset deficits in their accounts arising from the effects of the policy of price control at a time of rapidly rising costs.

My colleagues, who will speak later in the debate, will refer to legislative intentions in their own fields. I will confine myself to saying that we expect to have a busy programme here over the next year, touching on virtually every aspect of the life of Northern Ireland: Measures of law reform, such as the regulation of the solicitors' profession, and legislation to improve aspects of the housing situation, to deal with important questions of transport and communications and to improve our capacity to attract industrial investment.

These, and others, are fields on which preparations for legislation were going ahead before devolution, leading to proposals which we as an Executive can endorse. But, of course, since 1 January we have been getting down to the task of converting our own policies, as reflected by our Statement of Aims, into legislative shape. Accordingly, we will be making further statements to the Assembly about our legislative intentions in due course.

These, then, are our intentions in outline. But we appreciate that the confidence of this Assembly, which we seek, is not to be won by any declaration of future good intentions. We accept that we must convince the Assembly and the country that this course upon which we are set is truly in the interests of Northern Ireland and its people. Here I rest upon three simple questions which I would put to the House as a whole.

Virtually everyone of judgment now agrees that it has been a great source of weakness and instability to Northern Ireland over half-a-century that its Roman Catholic community, representing one-third of the population, has not played a commensurate part in the life and affairs of the Province. We can argue until the cows come home about whose fault that has been over all those years. We can go on attributing mutual blame up to and beyond the point where the rest of the world grows sick of us. All I know is that we have now found the means to work together. Are we now to say to that community, 'Democracy is simply majority rule, and if that means you are to sit in opposition for half-a-century more, it's just too bad'? I ask the opponents of all that we in this Executive represent, 'What is your answer?'

And I ask another question. A lot of people say they do not find this Constitution Act attractive or easy to stomach. It has a number of features which I personally regretted at the time and regret now. But what do we put in its place? And let us hear, please, some practical answers. Let us have the independent Ulster utopias properly costed. Let us learn how total integration is to be pushed through an unwilling Westminster Parliament. Let us hear precisely why a Council of Ireland, to which powers would be devolved only with our consent in this Assembly, is so insidious, while something described as an 'amalgamated Ireland,' in which Protestant domination of the North and Irish unification are miraculously accomplished side by side, is such a clever and thoroughly Loyalist idea. Let us be told how talk about defending democratic rights is to be reconciled with dark threats about blood and battle.

My third question is this: how is violence in Ireland ever to be ended if North and South cannot make common cause in the defence of democratic institutions? Through a Council of Ireland we have a means to ensure that such co-operation is maintained on a permanent and satisfactory basis. We shall acquire, for the first time, a formidable bargaining power which no Government in Dublin can ignore. We have seen this pattern already in Europe. No member nation of the EEC will agree to any movement in one area while its vital interests in another are being set at naught.

The significance of the unanimity rule in such an organisation is that progress in any direction is by agreement or not at all and that progress can be made only through recognising the interests of all the partners. I am in no way fearful that in a Council of Ireland the tradition I represent will be submerged. Indeed, the reverse will be true. Our basic position will be a fact with which any Government in Dublin will have to reckon. Our opponents have nothing to set against this gain but their old invocations of fear and prejudice: demand extradition, but close the gates of Ulster to the jurists who can discuss it. What on earth is the sense of it?

The plain fact is that the alternative to this Motion and to this Executive is a further period of utter confusion and uncertainty for Northern Ireland and her people. Truly, they do not deserve it. I believe they are crying out for less politics and more government.

Of course, we cannot promise what we cannot deliver. Law and order are not, for the time being, amongst our concerns, but we recognise that they remain the paramount concerns of countless thousands of people in our community.

No doubt from time to time views will be expressed here on these matters, but it is not for us, as an Executive, to reply to those views. We will answer here solely for those matters for which we are responsible to this Assembly. Because we do not wish to blur that line of constitutional responsibility we will offer advice to the Secretary of State only on those security issues which overlap or involve our own departmental responsibilities, such as the management of programmes in difficult areas or the protection of public installations.

There is no single, easy route back to peace and stability. But I believe that the resumption of real, constructive work in this Building can point the way to the community outside. They do not want to see us, I believe, producing hot air without end, vilifying and traducing each other. They want us to behave like grown men and women, like parliamentarians and democrats. They look to us for principled government and effective, fair-minded opposition. They demand of us good and just laws, firm and well directed administration. We must not fail them now. [*Hon. Members: Hear, hear*].

APPENDIX 4

Northern Ireland Administrations

March 1971: Brian Faulkner's Cabinet

Prime Minister: Brian Faulkner
Minister of Finance: Herbert Kirk
Minister of Home Affairs: Brian Faulkner
Minister of Health and Social Services: William Fitzsimmons
Minister of Education: Captain William Long
Minister of Agriculture: Harry West
Minister of Commerce: Robin Bailie
Minister of Development: Roy Bradford
Minister in and Leader of the Senate: J. L. O. Andrews
Minister of Community Relations: David Bleakley
Leader of the House of Commons: Nathaniel Minford
Minister of State, Ministry of Development: Nathaniel Minford
Minister of State, Ministry of Home Affairs: John Taylor
Minster of State, Ministry of Finance: Captain John Brooke

Attorney-General: Basil Kelly, QC

January 1974: Northern Ireland Executive

The Executive comprises 11 members as follows:
Chief Minister: Brian Faulkner (*Unionist*)
Deputy Chief Minister: Gerard Fitt M.P. (*SDLP*)
Legal Minister and Head of the Office of Law Reform: Oliver J. Napier (*Alliance*)
Minister of Information: John Lawson Baxter (*Unionist*)
Minister of the Environment: Roy H. Bradford (*Unionist*)

Minister of Housing, Local Government and Planning: J. Austin Currie (*SDLP*)

Minister of Health and Social Services: Patrick J. Devlin (*SDLP*)

Minister of Commerce: John Hume (*SDLP*)

Minister of Finance: Herbert V. Kirk (*Unionist*)

Minister of Education: W. Basil McIvor (*Unionist*)

Minister of Agriculture: Leslie J. Morrell (*Unionist*)

THE ADMINISTRATION

The Administration comprises the 11 members of the Executive plus the following:

Minister of Community Relations: Ivan Cooper (*SDLP*)

Minister of Manpower Services: Robert G. Cooper (*Alliance*)

Chief Whip: Major Lloyd Hall-Thompson (*Unionist*)

Minister of Planning and Co-ordination: Edward Kevin McGrady (*SDLP*)

APPENDIX 5

Key Dates

1921   18 February, born Helen's Bay, Co. Down
        7 June, Northern Ireland Parliament first meets
1935   St. Columba's College, Dublin—previously at local schools
1939   Queen's University, Belfast—law student
1940   Entered family business (resigned 1960)
1946   Member of Orange Order
         Joined Unionist Party and Young Unionist Movement
1947   Secretary Mid-Down Unionist Association
1949   Elected Unionist Member of Northern Ireland Commons
1951   Married Lucy Forsythe, Bangor, Co. Down
1956   Chief Whip
1959   Minister of Home Affairs
1963   Minister of Commerce
1969   January—resigned from O'Neill government
         May—Minister of Development in Chichester-Clarke government
1971   23 March—Prime Minister of Northern Ireland
         March—Speech on the Address suggests inter-party talks
      22 June—Ulster Jubilee Day, new proposals for participation by Opposition in Parliamentary Committees; anti-discrimination clause introduced in government contracts
       6 July—government agrees to purchase major share in Harland and Wolff, Ltd
      16 July—SDLP decide to set up rival Parliament
       9 August—Internment introduced
      20 August—White Paper, Record of Constructive Reform published by government
      27 September—tripartite talks with Mr. Heath and Mr. Lynch
      26 October—Green Paper on future development of Parliamentary government in Northern Ireland issued by Stormont

27 October—G. B. Newe (first Roman Catholic) appointed to Northern Ireland Government

1 December—Mater Hospital dispute resolved

23 December—Mr. Heath visits Northern Ireland

1972

March—Downing Street visits

March—Northern Ireland (Temporary Provisions) Act

24 March—final message to Northern Ireland people following Direct Rule

April—European Tour

25 September—Darlington Conference opens

October—Green Paper: The Future of Northern Ireland issued by British Government

1973

March—White Paper: Constitutional Future of Northern Ireland issued by British Government

28 June—Assembly Elections; Faulkner elected for South Down

18 July—Northern Ireland Constitution Act

31 July—first meeting of Northern Ireland Assembly

21 November—Executive-designate agreed between Unionist, SDLP and Alliance parties

6 December—Sunningdale Conference opens

14 December—Report to Northern Ireland Assembly

1974

1 January—Northern Ireland Executive takes office

24 January—statement outlining Executive policy

14 May—Vote on Sunningdale Agreement motion in Assembly

15 May—Ulster Workers' Council call general work stoppage

19 May—State of Emergency proclaimed

28 May—Brian Faulkner resigns and Direct Rule reimposed

Index